EDITH WHARTON'S
ETHAN FROME

EDITH WHARTON'S
ETHAN FROME

A Reference Guide

SUZANNE J. FOURNIER

Westport, Connecticut
London

Library of Congress Cataloging-in-Publication Data

Fournier, Suzanne J.
    Edith Wharton's Ethan Frome : a reference guide / Suzanne J. Fournier.
        p. cm.
    Includes bibliographical references (p.) and index.
    ISBN 0–313–33310–6 (alk. paper)
    1. Wharton, Edith, 1862–1937. Ethan Frome. I. Title.
    PS3545.H16E733   2006
    813'.52–dc22   2006001238

British Library Cataloguing in Publication Data is available.

Library of Congress Catalog Card Number: 2006001238
ISBN: 0–313–33310–6

First published in 2006

Praeger Publishers, 88 Post Road West, Westport, CT 06881
An imprint of Greenwood Publishing Group, Inc.
www.praeger.com

Printed in the United States of America

The paper used in this book complies with the
Permanent Paper Standard issued by the National
Information Standards Organization (Z39.48–1984).

10 9 8 7 6 5 4 3 2 1

For my mother, Shirley Fournier, and to the memory of my father, Raymond Fournier

CONTENTS

PREFACE

An unmistakable American work, *Ethan Frome* was written in the most European of cities as Edith Wharton embarked upon her life as an expatriate. An enthusiastic traveler since her childhood years abroad, Wharton and her husband Teddy spent the winter of 1907 settling into Paris' Faubourg Saint-Germain, the fashionable Left Bank neighborhood which would become her home for more than a decade. Her famous novel about a young farmer trapped in the frozen spaces of New England began there as a copy book exercise, a seven-page sketch written to help her improve her command of the French language. At the center of this story is a shy farmer named Hart, married to the sickly Anna but in love with her younger relation Mattie. That romantic triangle stirred Wharton's imagination again several years later, when she undertook a significantly more complex narrative about a protagonist she now called Ethan. Writing to a friend in the early months of 1911 about her progress on the novel, she commented on the pointed contrast between the novel's New England setting and her own Parisian milieu: "The scene is laid at Starkfield, Mass, and the nearest cosmopolis is called Shadd's Falls. It amuses me to do that décor in the rue de Varenne" (*Letters* 232). Far from her magnificent home in the Berkshires, Wharton devoted her best energies to evoking the life which she had observed for years in the villages and towns surrounding Lenox.

The novel which resulted is easily the best known of Wharton's long and distinguished career. Few would advance it as the most representative, however. Raised in the privilege and wealth of Old New York, Wharton is more readily identified with her novels of manners that weigh the values of the world which produced her. Works such as *The House of Mirth* and *The Custom of the Country* convey her fascination with the interplay between characters and classes in a rapidly changing social order. With trenchant irony, Wharton exposes the hollowness at the center of late nineteenth-century New York society as she chronicles its elaborate ceremonies and conventions. That glittering world would seem to have little in common with the setting of *Ethan Frome*, whose action is confined to a fading New England village and the hardscrabble farm on its outskirts. The scale of this 1911 work is similarly compressed, for the village of Starkfield lacks the defined society and fashionable gatherings of more emblematic Wharton novels.

Yet *Ethan Frome* stands at the center of the author's career, expressing the end of her long literary apprenticeship as well as the truth of her own experience. Reflecting on her slow and often diffident growth as a writer, Wharton places great emphasis on this short novel in her autobiography *A Backward Glance*. Although she savored the acclaim which had greeted *The House of Mirth* in 1905, she continued to struggle with her craft (and her understanding of her own abilities) until she attempted the story of an unhappily married Berkshire farmer. "I went on steadily trying to 'find out how to'; but I wrote two or three novels without feeling that I had made much progress. It was not until I wrote 'Ethan Frome' that I suddenly felt the artisan's full control of his implements" (209). The novel which she completed with such satisfaction had additional significance which she could not acknowledge in her memoir, for Wharton was experiencing a deepening crisis in her own marriage as she sketched Ethan's relationship with Zeena. She was also ending a short but passionate affair with the journalist Morton Fullerton as she developed the doomed romance between Ethan and Mattie. Coping with an unstable husband increasingly dependent on her, Wharton imagined a protagonist struggling vainly to escape an invalid spouse. Facing a lonely future in an unsatisfying marriage, she brought Ethan Frome's story to a violent climax on an icy hill and created one of the bleakest denouements in American literature.

Any estimation of the novel's importance quickly exceeds the bounds of biography, however. One of Wharton's most impressive works of fiction, *Ethan Frome* reveals her sure control of fictional form and language. Deftly incorporating ironic foreshadowing and extended patterns of imagery, it displays the techniques of her longer, more complex New York novels. Examining the pressure of circumstance on the lives of all three of its characters, it develops and refines a recurring theme in Wharton's oeuvre.

And this 1911 classic reflects major currents in modern American literature as well as its author's artistry. *Ethan Frome* remains a striking example of the realism project which reshaped the American novel in the last third of the nineteenth century, all the more memorably for its keen awareness of New England's local color movement. A twentieth-century narrative, it reveals the influence of literary naturalism in its fascination with environment and antici- pates the experimentation of modernism in its interiority and ambiguity. The expression of a volatile period in American fiction, *Ethan Frome* continues to reward close examination and debate.

The purpose of this reference guide is to provide a thorough introduction to the novel and its author. The guide is designed to serve a range of audi- ences, from the general reader interested in understanding the novel better to the graduate student seeking more specialized information about its critical reception. Undergraduates should find it a particularly helpful companion to *Ethan Frome*, illuminating the work's most important themes and symbols and analyzing its place in the American literary tradition. The scope of this reference work encompasses the novel's historical and cultural contexts; its structure, thought and craft; and the bibliography of criticism and theory devoted to it.

The opening chapter of the guide provides a valuable framework for con- sideration of *Ethan Frome*. The Introduction sketches the American society of Wharton's youth, approaching the Gilded Age as a time of dizzying change for a nation increasingly modern, urban and industrial. This historical overview encompasses Europe as well, contrasting the belle époque era which Wharton embraced in her new life as an expatriate with the ravaged years of World War I and the uneasy interregnum following the peace. The remainder of the Introduction consists of a comprehensive biographical essay. This discussion of Wharton's eventful life, spanning her upbringing in Old New York and her final years on the French Riviera, is centered on her growth as a writer. In her autobiography, Wharton tells how the publication of her first volume of stories (*The Greater Inclination*, 1899) brought her the home which she had been seeking for years: "The Land of Letters was henceforth to be my country, and I gloried in my new citizenship" (119). The Intro- duction's survey of her life is an attempt to convey her experience in this Land of Letters, concentrating on the books and friends and conversations so important to her sense of self throughout her career.

The next two chapters of this work look more closely at the novel and its origins. Chapter 1 offers a detailed synopsis of *Ethan Frome*, separating the story of the title character as a young man (Chapters I–IX) from the prologue and epilogue which convey his fate years after the "smash up." This section of the guide pays careful attention to the figure of the narrator, the visiting engineer determined to learn Ethan's past in wintry Starkfield. With its summary of plot, characterization and setting, Chapter 1 provides a firm basis for subsequent analysis of the novel. Chapter 2, "Texts," examines the various works and events which influenced Wharton's composition of *Ethan Frome*. The 1907 French exercise receives attention, as does the fatal sledding accident which occurred in Lenox on March 11, 1904 (and inspired the novel's climax). Chapter 2 considers two additional influences on the novel cited by Wharton in her introduction to the 1922 edition, Honore Balzac's story "La Grande Breteche" and Robert Browning's book-length poem *The Ring and the Book*. The remaining texts under discussion, including the private diary recording her affair with Morton Fullerton, illuminate the precarious state of her marriage as she completed *Ethan Frome* during the winter of 1911.

Chapter 3 of the guide is devoted to the literary contexts most meaningful to the novel, Nathaniel Hawthorne's romances and the local color realism of Sarah Orne Jewett and Mary Wilkins Freeman. Not surprisingly, these earlier works are firmly rooted in the New England countryside which dominates *Ethan Frome*. A disciplined reader who was thoroughly familiar with the converging streams of nineteenth-century American literature, Wharton expressed reservations about Hawthorne's achievement on more than one occasion. As she wrote her most successful novel of New England, however, she chose to pay homage to his fiction by incorporating aspects of his symbolic landscape and by naming Ethan and Zeena for two memorable characters from his works "Ethan Brand" and *The Blithedale Romance*. Perceiving modern New England as a depleted world, she evinced much less sympathy for late nineteenth-century regional writing. Insisting that the life which she witnessed in the Berkshires was "utterly unlike that seen through the rose-coloured spectacles of my predecessors, Mary Wilkins and Sarah Orne Jewett" (*Backward Glance* 293), Wharton intended *Ethan Frome* as a corrective to their work. Accordingly, Chapter 3 discusses the principles of local color realism and the distinguishing features of Jewett's and Freeman's fiction.

Chapter 4 marks the start of the guide's literary analysis, identifying and explaining the richest themes of *Ethan Frome*. Tracing the development of American naturalism in the 1890s, the chapter also discusses Wharton's fascination with Darwinian theory and her familiarity with the work of contemporaries such as Theodore Dreiser and Frank Norris. In *Ethan Frome*, Wharton tests the premises of their determinism by placing her protagonist under a "sky of iron" (63) and characterizing him as a prisoner of fate. An even more representative theme of Wharton's involves the habit of spectatorship apparent in Ethan from the first chapter of the novel, when he is depicted hiding in the shadows watching Mattie dance in a blaze of light. Ethan's passivity is a function of his desire to observe (or dream) rather than act, and Chapter 4 draws out the ways in which the novel undermines this posture. The final theme under consideration is the plight of women in Wharton's society. Emphasizing the vulnerability of Mattie, an orphaned young woman wholly unprepared for an independent life, the novel directs strong criticism at the assumptions of the world which has produced her. Notably less sympathetic toward the figure of Zeena, Wharton nonetheless treats her invalidism as another measure of the unsatisfying lives available to women at the turn of the century.

Chapter 5 furthers the reader's understanding of *Ethan Frome* by analyzing Wharton's narrative art. A strikingly economic novel, the work derives much of its meaning from its dense verbal texture. This section of the guide examines the range of concentrated images and ironic contrasts which extend and deepen characterization, setting and theme. Wharton draws on the world of nature throughout the novel, consistently associating her taciturn protagonist with the realities of winter, silence and death. The young woman he desires is aligned with spring, for Mattie seems to hold out to him the warmth and the color absent from his life. Other polarities which convey the predicament of Ethan and Mattie receive close attention, including the Romantic division between indoors and outdoors and the persistence of light/dark imagery. Another dimension of Wharton's technical achievement in the novel involves tone, and thus the chapter explores her deft use of ironic foreshadowing as she prepares her characters' fates.

Chapter 6 turns to the critical reception of the work, tracing the rising fortunes of *Ethan Frome* in Wharton's lifetime. A summary of reviews from the years 1911 to 1915 is a prominent feature of this chapter, with generous quotation from numerous newspapers and journals of the period. These contemporary reviews generally commend the novel as Wharton's finest work to date, citing its great power and the excellence of its design. More than one writer laments the unalleviated bleakness of the ending, however, and finds elements of classic Greek tragedy in the story of Ethan's romance with Mattie. This chapter also establishes the growing prominence of the novel in the twenty years following its publication, categorizing the early criticism which emerged in various studies of the modern novel and surveys of American literature. Although the novel was widely acclaimed as an American classic by the 1920s, several thoughtful essays arguing its limitations receive attention here as well. Owen and Donald Davis' dramatic adaptation of *Ethan Frome* in 1936 accounted for a final burst of commentary one year before Wharton's death, as critics seized the opportunity to honor the original novel as well as the Broadway production. These reviews confirm the novel's reputation by the end of the 1930s, as its author's masterpiece and an essential work of American literature.

The guide's closing chapter is a bibliographical essay of special value to students interested in further research. This essay charts the most significant developments in *Frome* scholarship since Wharton's death, organizing the many essays and books published into three distinct groups. The first is composed of papers from the 1940s and 1950s which concentrate on the historical and political implications of the novel. The most notable work in this category—and the single most influential essay ever published on *Ethan Frome*—is Lionel Trilling's "The Morality of Inertia" (1956). The second major group of essays was contributed by New Critics of the 1960s and 1970s, writers pursuing formal and technical questions about *Ethan Frome*. A neglected essay by Marius Bewley from this period receives close attention, in part because of its persuasive refutation of Trilling's charges against the novel. The third grouping, consisting of more theoretical essays and books written in the past twenty-five years, reflects a waning of scholarly interest in *Ethan Frome*. As feminist criticism began to dominate Wharton studies in the 1980s, *The House of Mirth* and *The Custom of the Country* quickly rose to prominence. The bibliographical essay discusses the most significant feminist writing on *Ethan Frome*, concluding with a brief review of secondary resources.

INTRODUCTION

A REMARKABLE LIFE

Edith Newbold Jones was born during the Civil War, and she died on the eve of World War II. In the course of her lifetime, the United States shed the vestiges of a rural republic and emerged as an industrial world power. The privileged New York society which produced Wharton changed dramatically as well, adopting the excesses of the Gilded Age and coarsening further during the Jazz Age. The writer described by Edmund Wilson as a "passionate social prophet" of American literature honed her craft in Europe and spent her most productive years in France, far from the manners and mores she chronicled (*Wound and the Bow* 160). A strong and fiercely independent woman, she nonetheless scorned the suffragette movement of the 1920s and favored the title "Mrs. Wharton" all the years following her painful divorce. Wharton nursed her young vocation as the American Renaissance drew to a close, and gained her first significant readership when Henry Wadsworth Longfellow recommended a poem of hers for publication. She refined her fictional style during the flowering of literary realism and naturalism and continued writing in unwavering voice throughout the experimental years of High Modernism. To the end of her life, in a world very different from the one which shaped her, Wharton cultivated her art with energy and conviction.

THE CULTURE

The Emergence of Modern America

Many of the changes which reshaped the country at the end of the nineteenth century were inextricably tied to the American Industrial Revolution. Although industry was established in American society years before the Civil War, its explosive growth occurred during the period of Reconstruction. The historian Sean Cashman notes, "Between 1865 and 1901 the American Industrial Revolution transformed the United States from a country of small and isolated communities scattered across 3 million square miles of continental territory into a compact economic and industrial unit. Thus, the rural republic of Lincoln and Lee became the industrial empire of Roosevelt and Bryan" (12). A second-rate industrial power in 1860, the United States overtook England, France and Germany by 1890. The value of American manufactured goods in the decade swelled until it nearly equaled the total of goods produced by all three European countries. The United States' national wealth grew rapidly as well, nearly doubling between 1890 and 1900. Modern finance capitalism developed on Wall Street as industrial capitalism matured and robber barons such as Andrew Carnegie and Cornelius Vanderbilt sought places to invest their enormous profits. John D. Rockefeller's swift rise to control of the country's oil supply through Standard Oil confirmed the power of the business monopolies in the Gilded Age (Tipple 21–23).

The success of the American industry depended on the accompanying revolutions in transportation and communication. The first transcontinental railroad was approved by Congress during the Civil War, when the Union Pacific and Central Pacific companies began working to connect the country. In a moment of great significance nationwide, the two railroad lines joined in May 1869 at Promontory Point in Utah. Covering 35,000 miles in 1865, the railroad grew exponentially for the next thirty years, reaching close to 200,000 miles in 1900. This extension of the American railroad was critical to the new industrial economy, for trains linked city and countryside by delivering freight in the form of raw materials and manufactured goods. The transcontinental railroad sped the settlement of the West as well, attracting miners, ranchers and farmers in record numbers. In the last thirty years of the nineteenth century, these groups of pioneers staked their claims to more land than had been settled in the previous 250 years (Cashman 256). The result was the highly symbolic closing of the American frontier in 1890, when the Bureau of the Census announced that a defined frontier line could no longer be discerned in the West.

Sweeping changes in the way Americans began to communicate with each other seemed to shrink the country even further. The inventors Thomas Alva Edison and Alexander Graham Bell influenced many of the technological advances of the late nineteenth century, improving the lives of Wharton and her contemporaries as they aided the captains of industry. Edison helped to transform the field of communication by enlarging and extending the capacity of the telegraph in use throughout the Civil War. His invention of the incandescent light bulb in 1879 led to the 1882 opening of the first central power station in New York and the development of a reliable source of alternating current for the 1893 World's Fair in Chicago. Bell patented the first telephone in 1876, and the American Telephone and Telegraph Company was incorporated less than ten years later. By the turn of the century, more than one million phones were in use throughout the United States. Wharton was delighted by this invention and used it so regularly that she became indignant when she realized that a house which she had rented for the summer of 1914 was not equipped with a phone (Lewis 7).

The automobile introduced in the early 1900s changed Wharton's life even more dramatically. The invention of the gasoline engine made the "horseless carriage" a modern reality, after earlier unsuccessful attempts to fuel prototypes with steam or electricity. The first viable motor car appeared in 1903, and more than sixty American companies were producing automobiles by 1910. Already making cars by 1908, Henry Ford introduced the fabled Model T a year later (with a price tag of $950) and sold 168,000 within the next five years. The 1914 opening of his Michigan plant—equipped with the first electric conveyor belt—made the American car more widely available (and more affordable). Wharton began riding in cars as early as 1903 in Italy, and she owned her first automobile by her forty-second birthday in 1904. (The Whartons' purchase of a second car that year, a Pope-Hartford that boasted ten horsepower, was an event that merited attention in a local newspaper.) The author began her 1908 travelogue *A Motor-Flight through France* with the exultant claim, "The motor-car has restored the romance of travel" (1). Like a rapidly growing number of Americans, Wharton regarded the shining automobile as a source of freedom and even power.

Quick to embrace many of the age's technological advances, the writer deplored other, more fundamental changes wrought by the Industrial Revolution. The same forces of urbanization and immigration which ensured the success of American industry transformed the United States which Wharton knew in her youth. Cities grew at a volatile rate in the last third of the nineteenth century, as extended rail lines helped to concentrate the population near heavily industrial centers in the Northeast and the Midwest. By 1900, more than one third of all Americans lived in city neighborhoods rather than on farms. Wharton's New York more than tripled its population between 1850 and 1900, and jumped from three million to five million citizens by 1910. The number of large cities rose as sharply in these postwar years: by 1900, there were fifty American cities with populations exceeding one hundred thousand citizens.

Three massive waves of immigration, each larger than the one before and drawing from different areas of Europe, helped to swell these hastily constructed cities and to fill out the labor force (Cashman 87). Population growth in nineteenth-century Europe produced shortages of food and work which made the promises of the American Industrial Revolution all the more compelling. The result was an influx of more than ten million immigrants between 1860 and 1890 and another fifteen million immigrants between 1890 and 1914. Richard Hofstadter comments that the American living in one of the great urban centers felt "outnumbered and overwhelmed" by so many newcomers from unfamiliar areas of southern and eastern Europe (*Age of Reform* 176).

The modern cities which struggled to absorb these numbers were the focus of numerous reform efforts, beginning in the 1890s and continuing through the Progressive Era. The effects of unregulated industrialization and urbanization throughout the Gilded Age were vast wealth for some—the one percent of the population which enjoyed more than half the national wealth—and abject poverty for many more. "American cities, springing into life out of mere villages, often organized around nothing but the mill, the factory, or the railroad, peopled by a heterogeneous and mobile population, and drawing upon no settled governing classes for administrative experience, found the pace of their growth far out of proportion to their capacity for management" (Hofstadter, *Age of Reform* 174). The social fragmentation which resulted from so much rapid undirected growth was exacerbated by rampant corruption in municipal and state governments alike. Well-educated men and women of the urban middle class responded by leading reform movements aimed at improving living conditions in overcrowded cities, eliminating child labor, regulating workdays for women and enforcing safety regulations in factories. Wharton's 1907 novel *The Fruit of the Tree* reflects her sympathy for these reformers in its portrayal of a heroine combating untenable labor practices in a New York mill. Although the novel lacks the urgency—and the influence—of more famous muckraking works such as Jacob Riis' *How the Other Half Lives* (1893) and Upton Sinclair's *The Jungle* (1906), it expresses her identification with the growing number of Americans intent on restoring a misshapen society.

Wharton deeply admired the energy and the vision of Theodore Roosevelt, a member of her patrician class who embodied the spirit of the era. Drawn to public life in the 1880s, he completed vigorous turns as Police Commissioner of New York City and Assistant Secretary of the Navy before serving heroically in the Spanish American War and becoming governor of New York in 1898. Advanced to the Vice Presidency by New York party bosses unable to manipulate him, he entered the White House in 1901 (following the assassination of William McKinley) and immediately began using the powers of his office on behalf of progressive reform (Goldman 162–63). The changes which he and his administration achieved in the next eight years ranged from regulation of the railroads and creation of pure food and drug laws to conservation of public lands. Contending with the vast power of the trusts and monied interests, he provided modern America with a model of "regulated capitalism" that would guide Woodrow Wilson and (especially) Franklin Delano Roosevelt (DiNunzio 15). In the range of his intellectual interests as well as his commitment to his country, he came to express Wharton's ideal of leadership. The two became fast friends by the start of Roosevelt's second term, when he greeted her at a formal dinner with the words, "Well, I *am* glad to welcome to the White House some one to whom I can quote 'The Hunting of the Snark' without being asked what I mean!" (Lewis 145).

An Unquiet Century

By the end of Roosevelt's presidency, Wharton had embarked on the expatriate life which she would lead until her death in 1937. She moved to Paris in the heady years preceding World War I and never considered returning to America during the fifty-two months of fighting in Europe. In her autobiography *A Backward Glance*, she evokes the idyllic summer of 1914 as she recalls when she first learned of the June 28th assassination of two members of the Hapsburg royal family:

It was a perfect summer day; brightly dressed groups were gathered at tea-tables beneath the overhanging boughs, or walking up and down the flower-bordered turf. Broad bands of blue forget-me-nots edged the shrubberies, old-fashioned *corbeilles* of yellow and bronze wall-flowers dotted the lawn, the climbing roses were budding on the pillars of the porch. Outside in the quiet street stood a long line of motors, and on the lawn and about the tea-tables there was a happy stir of talk. An exceptionally gay season was stirring to its close, the air was full of new literary and artistic emotions, and that dust of ideas with which the atmosphere of Paris is always laden sparkled like motes in the sun. (336)

Hearing on this golden afternoon that a young Serbian student had killed Archduke Franz Ferdinand and his wife, Wharton was distracted only briefly from discussion of a new play in Paris and an exhibition at the Louvre. During the next five weeks of diplomatic sorties involving a widening circle of countries, she enjoyed a vacation in Spain and completed plans for an extended stay in the British countryside (to begin in August 1914). Like everyone else on the continent at the end of the belle époque, Wharton underestimated the significance of the events in Bosnia and was wholly unprepared for the devastation of the Great War.

Europeans (and Americans) had good reason to be surprised by the August declarations of war which followed the mobilization of troops in one country after another. No major war had occurred in the continent for more than one hundred years, and no fighting had taken place in Western Europe since 1871. Although the great powers had continued to amass weapons and soldiers in growing numbers into the new century—prompting the Russian Tsar to deplore the "accelerating arms race" in 1899—an elaborate system of treaties and alliances remained in place in 1914 (Keegan 17). Historian John Keegan points to the "interdependence of nations" in Europe at the outbreak of war, emphasizing the spirit of internationalism fostering collaboration in areas ranging from the practical to the philosophical and intellectual. "Europe in the summer of 1914 enjoyed a peaceful productivity so dependent on international exchange and co-operation that a belief in the impossibility of general war seemed the most conventional of wisdoms" (10). When the outbreak of war between Austria-Hungary and Serbia appeared increasingly likely by late July, Europeans spoke confidently of a short contest. Governments across the continent were surprised by the outpouring of patriotic sentiment following the mobilization of troops and by the sheer number of volunteers eager to enlist before the skirmish ended.

The world war that ensued between the Central Powers (Austria-Hungary, Germany) and the Allies (France, Russia, Britain) represented such a complete break with the past that it has been described as "the crossing of a historical frontier" (Hobsbawm, *Empire* 326). The novelist Henry James's words of disbelief and pain at the onset of war capture this sense of profound disjuncture between the nineteenth and twentieth centuries:

The plunge of civilization into this abyss of blood and darkness by the wanton feat of those two infamous autocrats is a thing that so gives away the whole long age during which we have supposed the world to be, with whatever abatement, gradually bettering, that to have to take it all now for what the treacherous years were all the while really making for and *meaning* is too tragic for any words. (*Letters of Henry James* 384)

The war expected to end in six weeks' time instead continued through November 1918 and engulfed all but six European states (and the United States by 1917). The escalating conflict became a war of attrition, with opposing sides positioned within the first five months of fighting in a line of trenches extending eventually from the coast of Belgium to the border of Switzerland. The battles which occurred resulted in unprecedented losses for an entire generation of soldiers: on one day of fighting in the 1916 Battle of the Somme, sixty thousand men were killed or wounded (Fussell 13). The vast scale of this battle—as well as the rising deaths—was unforeseeable before 1914. All of the major powers suffered punishing losses, and Serbia itself sacrificed fifteen percent of its population to World War I. The toll of destruction at war's end included ten million dead, twenty million wounded and three hundred billion dollars' worth of the world's treasures ruined.

The Europe in which Wharton spent the final years of her life was changed irremediably by this war and by the "hope-smothering defects" of the peace treaty signed at Versailles on June 28, 1919 (Kennedy 6). The failure of President Woodrow Wilson to form a League of Nations out of the rubble of the fighting was merely one source of the deepening strain in European politics through the outbreak of a yet greater war, World War II. What Versailles supplied instead of a peacekeeping body was a new map of Europe, reflecting the collapse of dynasties in Germany, Austria and Russia as a result of the war and the creation of five different nation-states. Efforts by the victors to impose draconian measures on a defeated Germany, as well as to contain the Bolshevism of the 1917 revolution, resulted in a destabilized Europe vulnerable to fascism and totalitarianism (Hobsbawm, *Extremes* 31–32). The severe economic depression of the 1930s—the worst afflicting the West since industrialization—hastened the rise of Adolf Hitler in Germany and other ambitious demagogues elsewhere. Keegan's view of these developments as the continuing legacy of World War I is a common one: "Less than twenty years after the end of the Great War, the 'war to end wars' as it had come to be called at the nadir of hopes for its eventual conclusion, Europe was once again gripped by the fear of a new war, provoked by the actions and ambitions of war lords more aggressive than any known to the old world of the long nineteenth-century peace" (9). Dying in France in 1937, Wharton was only too aware of the fissures in the European landscape of the twentieth century and fearful of their inevitable, violent consequences.

THE LIFE

A Proper Upbringing

Edith Wharton began her life in Old New York, and she was raised in a society which she later described as "safe, guarded, monotonous" (*Backward Glance* 7). She was born on January 24, 1862, to Lucretia (Stevens) Rhinelander and George Frederic Jones, at 14 West Twenty-Third Street near fashionable Washington Square. She was the third child and only daughter of George and Lucretia; the ages of her brothers Frederic (16) and Harry (11) at her birth meant that her upbringing was largely similar to that of an only child of older parents. The Jones and Stevens families were part of the city's patrician class, with roots in New York since the seventeenth century and origins in England and Holland. A favorite ancestor of Edith's was her great grandfather Ebenezer Stevens, a towering figure who participated in the Boston Tea Party, rose to the rank of General in the Revolutionary War and later prospered in the East India merchant trade.

By the nineteenth century, General Stevens' descendants led quieter lives regulated by the inherited traditions and obligations of the American leisure class. George Frederic Jones was the youngest surviving child of a prosperous family. After completing the Grand Tour with his father in 1838, he prepared for the life of a gentleman by earning a degree from Columbia College in

"The Literature and Scientific Course." In 1844 he married Lucretia Rhinelander, the eldest daughter of a family plunged into financial difficulties after the early death of the father. (The poverty which the family experienced was distinctly genteel, for the children's proper education continued unabated and the young Rhinelanders retained their own horses and riding habits [Lewis 11].) Lucretia suffered the indignity of a homemade gown and ill-fitting borrowed slippers for her debut in society, but she was soon rewarded with the romance of a secret courtship with George Frederic Jones. Discouraged from seeing a "poor" Rhinelander on the outskirts of the city, George wooed Lucretia one summer by sailing to her at dawn in a rowboat equipped with a bed quilt sail lashed to an improvised mast. Over-coming the reservations of the Jones family, the two married and took their place in the close world of "old New York cousinships" that formed polite society (*Backward Glance* 58). Dividing their time between New York and Newport, they enjoyed a well-appointed life of social calls, formal dinners, charitable events and evenings at the opera.

Many years later, Wharton began her autobiography by describing a child's winter walk down Fifth Avenue with her father. Her affection for her hand-some father shapes this passage, and he holds a place of honor throughout *A Backward Glance*. George Frederic Jones and his only daughter came to share a passion for books, an enthusiasm for travel, a delight in nature (especially gardens) and an appreciation for art. Edith's relations with her mother were more complicated, and anecdotes about the formidable Lucretia Jones abound in Wharton biographies and letters. Young Edith was fascinated by her mother, who compensated for her shabby debutante gown by ordering the finest clothes from Paris each season and cultivating a reputation as the best-dressed woman in New York. Devoted to her older sons, Lucretia was exacting in her dealings with her only daughter and quick to express her disapproval. When twelve-year-old Edith showed her an early literary effort which began with the exchange, " 'Oh, how do you do, Mrs. Brown?' said Mrs. Tomkins. 'If only I had known you were going to call I should have tidied up the drawing room,' " Lucretia gave the work a cur-sory glance and reminded her daughter that " 'drawing rooms are always tidy' " (*Backward Glance* 73). As a child, Edith found her "inscrutable" mother harder to please than God ("Life" 1074).

The Joneses' long sojourn in Europe became another defining feature of Edith's childhood. Like many of his class whose incomes were tied to New York real estate, George Frederic chose to escape the postwar recession of the late 1860s and 1870s by renting his homes in New York and Newport and taking his family abroad. Edith was four years old when her parents left the United States for Italy, and her first years in Europe stirred her young ima-gination and sparked her lifelong fascination with foreign sights and ancient history. The family enjoyed a sunny winter in Rome before embarking on a much more adventurous trip to Spain, where they followed an itinerary inspired by George Frederic's reading of Washington Irving's *The Alhambra*. Wharton would later describe this exotic pilgrimage vividly and claim that it was the source of her "incurable passion for the road" (*Backward Glance* 31). The family also spent several years in Paris, where young Edith enjoyed the spectacle associated with the final days of the Second Empire and began acquiring fluency in the first of several new languages. George Frederic and Lucretia left France at the outbreak of the Franco-Prussian War, choosing to spend the summer of 1870 at the resort Bad Wildbad in Germany's Black Forest. There, Edith contracted typhoid fever and nearly died before her parents found a Russian doctor capable of treating the disease effectively. Following a long convalescence in Germany, Edith returned to Italy with her family and spent most of 1871 in Florence.

The Jones family's homecoming in 1872 was discomfiting for ten-year-old Edith. During her years abroad, she had developed an appreciation for beauty and an interest in architecture which helped to define her keen aesthetic sense as she grew older. Unaccustomed to the bustle and clamor of New York in the busy 1870s, she longed to return to the European cities she had visited. The family brownstone was a disappointment after the hotels and villas of France and Italy, the neighboring city streets dull and undistinguished. Summers in Newport at the family home Pencraig offered more beautiful vistas—and thus more pleasure—but Edith continued to press her father throughout her adolescence to arrange another trip to the continent. Her biographer R. W. B. Lewis has commented on the lasting influence of her early years abroad:

Europe was also a variety of styles of living, dressing, eating, talking. It was the experience of a great variety of manners; as a result, Edith would look with a particularly acute and probing eye at the manners of her own American society. It was above all the almost painful discovery of unfamiliar physical beauty, beauty of landscape and garden, of forest and country road, of village and cathedral. Ugliness, she said, always rather frightened her. (19)

The child's dismay at her first sight of New York harbor in 1872 would overtake the adult each time she returned to America from Europe, until she eventually chose to remain abroad for decades at a time. This preference for European culture which Edith formed in her early years thus directed her restless steps throughout her life, for she considered herself an "exile" in the United States from the age of ten ("Life" 1081).

The Fascinating World of Books

Wharton's life of storytelling also began in these formative years abroad. Uninterested in Mother Goose or Hans Christian Anderson, she favored Greek mythology at an early age and relished stories of "grown up" gods and goddesses on Mount Olympus. She enjoyed creating her own tales even more, and it was in Paris at the age of six that she first devised the ritual of "making up" that satisfied her desire to tell stories. She required a book, preferably the same edition of *The Alhambra* which guided her family through romantic Spain and room to pace furiously as she turned upside-down pages and pretended to read her newest story aloud. The mystery of these pages which she could fill with her own words appealed to the child so deeply that she resisted her father's initial efforts to teach her to read. When she did learn to read, however, she began to devour the books available to her, for they extended the possibilities of the "secret story-world" in which she lived ("Life" 1077).

Long before Edith fell ill in Germany and devoted the slow months of her recovery to reading, Lucretia was becoming concerned about these solitary habits of her unusual daughter. As Edith grew, her mother made several futile efforts to call her away from the world of books. When Lucretia withdrew proper writing paper, Edith learned to hoard the brown wrapping paper which arrived with parcels and to take pleasure in filling the long strips with her stories. When Lucretia asked to examine every work of fiction which her daughter wanted to read, Edith obediently submitted novels for her mother's approval beforehand and continued doing so until she was married. Her mother set no limit on other genres, however, and Edith gleefully laid siege to her father's library as soon as the family returned to New York. In the history and philosophy and poetry which she read, she began to claim for herself the education which her tutors had not provided. She had few books of her own, but she acquired an impressive knowledge of the classics by reading widely in her father's library and in her brother Harry's college texts (Wolff 44).

At the same time, Edith was beginning to cultivate her "secret garden," her term in *A Backward Glance* for her career as a writer. Her second attempt at a novel (following her short-lived examination of Mrs. Tomkins' messy drawing room) was an 1876 satire of English romance entitled *Fast and Loose*, completed under the pen name David Olivieri (Colquitt, "Visions and Revisions" 250). A distinction of this piece was the clever appendix which Edith supplied of "reviews" deploring the novel and highlighting its many deficiencies.[1] The only person permitted to read *Fast and Loose* was Emelyn Washburn, a slightly older friend who shared her passion for Goethe and Dante and steadfastly encouraged her writing. Emelyn's father, Reverend Washburn, rector of the church which the Jones family attended, offered Edith the use of his library (a rich supplement to her father's) and of his typewriter. Serving as her mentor for several years, he read the poetry she had begun to write and was as supportive as his daughter when Edith expressed a desire to become a professional writer. The first money she ever earned—$50 in 1877 for her translation of a poem by the German poet Heinrich Karl Brugsch—was the result of Dr. Washburn's submission of her work under his own signature. Soon after this success, her parents arranged for the private publication of Edith's poems and translations in a chapbook entitled *Verses.*

A Debutante in Old New York

Edith was not permitted to devote all of her time to literary pursuits, however. As her formal debut neared she often spent her mornings with Anna Bahlmann, the finishing governess hired to prepare her to assume her place in society and her afternoons with her mother in the family carriage. She became a debutante a year earlier than usual, explaining in her autobiographical fragment "Life and I" that her parents arranged this event when she was seventeen out of concern over her painful shyness, her intellectual bent and her indifference toward people her own age (1092). Her biographer Shari Benstock suggests that George Frederic's financial worries and accompanying poor health may have been stronger factors in the choice of date for this debut, for New York's "old money" was struggling in the heady economic climate following the postwar recession. As the nouveau riche amassed fortunes (and power) in the stock market during the Gilded Age, older families dependent on real estate income suffered financial setbacks (Benstock 40–41). Fearing reduced circumstances which might blight Edith's prospects for marriage, Lucretia arranged a debutante ball for her daughter in 1879, at the Fifth Avenue mansion of her friend Mrs. Levi Morton. Spared a larger fete in the more customary setting of Delmonico's, Edith was able to enjoy her evening visiting with her many Jones and Rhinelander cousins and dancing with her brother Harry's friends.

Edith circulated in New York society for only one season before accompanying her parents to Europe when her father's health worsened. She maintained a busy schedule of luncheons, dinners and theater engagements during that first season and later attracted a lively complement of houseguests to Pencraig for activities ranging from tennis and archery to boat races in the bay and rides along Ocean Drive. Self-conscious and diffident in her dealings with the gentlemen around her, Edith nonetheless acquired at least one determined suitor following her debut. Harry Stevens spent the early summer of 1880 at Edith's side in Newport, followed the Jones family to Bar Harbor when they visited her brother Frederick and his family and continued on to the continent in 1881. Edith's engagement to Stevens was announced in August 1882 but it lasted only a few months. Harry's mother, a grocer's daughter now in possession of a large fortune, had been rebuffed by Lucretia and the Rhinelanders in her earlier efforts to gain entrance to Old New York society. A flamboyant member of the rich upstart class which would figure prominently in Edith's best novels, Mrs. Paran Stevens would not permit her son's marriage into the circle which had resisted her overtures.

The death of George Frederic Jones in 1882 overshadowed all other losses for Edith. His rapid decline dictated the family's travel to Europe in the fall of 1880, when his doctors recommended that he seek the gentler climate of the Riviera. Initially hopeful that her father would regain his vigor abroad, Edith delighted in his gifts of Ruskin's *Stones of Venice* and *Walks in Florence* and used the books to plan her own rambles through Italian city streets. George Frederic weakened steadily, however, and he never recovered from the stroke which he suffered early in 1882. In *A Backward Glance*, Wharton comments on the pain she felt as she watched her paralyzed father slip away: "I am still haunted by the look in his dear blue eyes, which had followed me so tenderly for nineteen years, and now tried to convey the goodbye messages he could not speak. Twice in my life I have been at the death-bed of some one I dearly loved, who has vainly tried to say a last word to me; and I doubt if life holds a subtler anguish" (88).[2] Her father died at Cannes on March 15, 1862, and was buried in the family vault there. Lucretia and her daughter returned to Pencraig in mourning and settled within the year into a new home in Washington Square.

Edith participated dutifully in the New York/Newport seasons following the loss of her father and the end of her short-lived engagement, finding herself with little time for reading or writing. During her now-annual visit to Bar Harbor in the summer of 1883, however, she formed an acquaintance with a member of her class who shared her love of literature and ideas. In her meetings with Walter Van Rensselaer Berry in Maine, she discovered a companion who satisfied her deep need for conversation about the authors and the works that absorbed her. A graduate of Harvard who had recently completed an eighteen-month tour of Europe, Walter Berry was reading for the Washington Bar when he met Edith. Another distant Rhinelander cousin of Lucretia's, he spent so much time with Edith at Bar Harbor that summer that she hoped he would soon propose to her. Lewis suggests that although Berry enjoyed Edith's company—and shared her passion for literature—he found richer, less serious women better prospects for marriage (49). Although Walter Berry disappeared from Edith's life for more than a dozen years after disappointing her, he would eventually assume the role of her closest friend for three decades.

Courtship and Marriage

During that same visit to Bar Harbor, Edith met Edward Robbins Wharton of Boston and began a leisurely courtship which did lead to marriage. Thirteen years older than she, "Teddy" Wharton was a well-bred bachelor who had been comfortably settled with his mother and sister on Beacon Street for some time. Unlike Walter Berry, Teddy had no vocation and shared none of Edith's intellectual and literary interests. An 1873 graduate of Harvard, he finished his junior year tenth from the bottom of his class with an average of forty-five and showed little aptitude for any subject other than natural history (Benstock 53). Handsome and popular, he enjoyed the life of a gentleman and favored outdoor activities such as camping, hunting and riding. Lucretia considered Teddy an excellent suitor for her daughter and took steps from the first summer at Bar Harbor to encourage his interest. Fittingly enough, the engagement ring which he eventually offered Edith was composed of Lucretia's jewels as well as his own band of diamonds (Benstock 58).

Unlikely as the marriage between Edith and Teddy now seems, she accepted his proposal gladly in 1885. Still unmarried six years after her debut, she was growing concerned about her prospects for her own home and her own place in society. In Teddy she found a kind and attentive companion of similar breeding who was prepared to leave Boston society for life with her in New York. His lively wit and ease with others in their circle helped disguise her continuing shyness and insecurity. Like her, he was devoted to animals and fondly indulgent of the small dogs which she favored as pets. He shared her enthusiasm for Europe, and would soon spend four months of each year traveling abroad with her (and smoothing her passage through foreign terrain and uncomfortable hotels). Teddy and Edith's marriage was strained from the beginning by a lack of physical intimacy, however, and within three weeks of their April 1885 wedding they settled into a relationship which was friendly rather than passionate. Her effort to learn from Lucretia beforehand "what being married was like" had been angrily rebuffed, leading her to write years later that her mother's failure to supply her with the simplest information about sexual relations "did more than anything else to falsify and misdirect my whole life" ("Life" 1088). The incomplete nature of Edith's marriage—and its increasingly obvious inequality—would inspire a long series of unsatisfying unions in her fiction.

During the first years of the Whartons' life together, however, Edith had neither time nor confidence to nurture her vocation. As Teddy had an allowance of only two thousand dollars a year, they depended on her trust fund for income. Unable to buy their own home at the start of their marriage, they settled for eight months of each year in Pencraig Cottage on Lucretia's property in Newport. Although Teddy threw himself into each new social season with enthusiasm, Edith was increasingly dismayed by the garishness of the rapidly changing city by the sea. She preferred to concentrate on planning each year's journey to Europe, and a highlight of her young married life was an 1888 cruise around the Mediterranean with Teddy and their cultured friend James Van Alen. She regarded this trip as her opportunity to explore the ancient world which had fascinated her for years, and she developed an itinerary inspired by Odysseus' journey from Troy to Ithaca. She delighted in reading Homer's *Odyssey* aloud at night as the yacht made its way from Algiers to Italy, and she moved energetically through the often rough countryside as the three completed more than forty stops in four months.

The notebook which she kept during this ambitious voyage has been published recently as *The Cruise of the Vanadis*, and it provides the first example of her distinctive travel writing.

Soon after Wharton returned in triumph from this cruise, she learned that she was the beneficiary of a sizeable bequest from an eccentric elderly cousin. Her legacy permitted her to purchase Land's End, a Newport property near the cliffs of Ocean Drive. Eleanor Dwight suggests that the move from Pencraig Cottage to the other side of the city meant much more to Wharton than independence from Lucretia: "Land's End was Wharton's first real home of her own, acquired at a time when she was struggling to create a new self" (42). Owning this home bolstered Wharton's identity as a writer, for it led to her collaboration with a talented young architect who launched his career in fashionable society by renovating Land's End under her close supervision. Discovering that Ogden Codman shared her distaste for prevailing Victorian notions of décor, Wharton proposed that they publish their ideas about interior decoration. The result of their efforts was her first book, *The Decoration of Houses* (1897).

Gratified by the success of this work, Wharton was even more pleased by Scribner's offer to publish a collection of her short stories. Although her poems and stories had been appearing in *Scribner's Magazine* since the end of the 1880s, she was not yet writing with regularity or confidence. For more than a dozen years after her marriage, Wharton suffered a number of debilitating symptoms which left her weak and unable to work for months at a time. Prone to bronchial infections and respiratory problems after her childhood bout with typhoid, she was troubled by the dampness of Newport weather and increasingly anxious to leave the city each winter. Her lifelong habit of throwing herself energetically into each new project (house, garden, book) accounted for other bouts of illness and fatigue, as she was inclined to overextend herself to the point of collapse in order to meet a deadline or complete an important task. Unable to overcome the lassitude which invariably followed her illnesses, she spent the summer and fall of 1898 resting in Philadelphia under a doctor's care.[3] As she regained her strength, she completed her first volume of fiction, *The Greater Inclination* (1899).

ENTERING THE LAND OF LETTERS

The publication of this work at century's end strengthened Wharton's resolve to take her place in a community of writers and thinkers, outside the narrow confines of New York society. She comments in *A Backward Glance* that the appearance of *The Greater Inclination* awakened her soul and opened a world to her, the "Land of Letters" which she had been seeking vainly for years (119). A serious reader married to someone wholly uninterested in books and ideas, she eventually formed a circle of close friends who shared her passion for the life of the mind. Early in her marriage, a family friend whom she called one of her "Awakeners" (a term used interchangeably in the autobiography for books or people) guided her through a rigorous course of study composed of books which she had never encountered on her own. In his long conversations with Wharton about authors such as Darwin and Huxley, Egerton Winthrop gave form to her reading and answered her need for conversation about topics that mattered. Long after her career began to flourish, Wharton drew energy for her writing from similar conversations with friends about the books she was reading.

Wharton relied on regular visits and frequent correspondence with her friends, for they offered her much more than intellectual conversation. Married to an affable but dull husband and deprived of close ties to her remaining family, she placed her friends at the center of her life and experienced continuity through her relations with them. The international lawyer Walter Berry became her great companion and confidante for more than thirty years, reentering her life as she was struggling to complete *The Decoration of Houses*. The one reader she trusted implicitly, he encouraged her throughout her career and commented on each work in progress before she submitted it for publication. The French writer Paul Bourget became another member of her widening circle of friends in America and Europe after meeting her in Newport in 1893. An inveterate traveler, he and his wife Minnie took long European trips with the Whartons and remained close to Edith after her divorce from Teddy in 1913. The friends who formed the tightest bonds with Wharton over the long years of her career were distinguished by their love of art or history or travel, and Charles Eliot Norton was no exception. She visited his summer home in the Berkshires as often as she could, and was grateful for the lively interest which he took in her fiction. His daughter Sally formed her own acquaintance with the writer after admiring her stories in *Scribner's Magazine*, and she became one of Wharton's closest woman friends for more than twenty years.

As this "floating court of friends" took shape and grew stronger (Bell 65), Wharton was discovering a rich focus for her writing in her annual trips to Italy. Her favorite destination since childhood, it inspired her first novel and her first two forays into travel writing. Her special interest in Italy was not the Renaissance but the *settecento*, and she became an expert on the art and architecture of this period with the help of Winthrop. Traveling through the Tuscan countryside every year—often with Winthrop or the Bourgets as well as Teddy—she ignored the routes charted in guidebooks and instead explored historic villages and churches of her own choosing. In this way, she made an impressive artistic discovery in the spring of 1894: a set of six terra cotta figures by della Robbia rendering scenes from the Passion, formerly attributed to a lesser known seventeenth-century artist. These figures were distributed among twenty hillside chapels near a monastery outside the small village of San Vivaldo, and Wharton identified their creator by comparing them to the work of della Robbia in the Bargello. Confident of her judgment, she brought a professional photographer to San Vivaldo and submitted his pictures to the Academy in Florence. Soon after her discovery was verified, she wrote enthusiastically to her editor Edward Burlingame at Scribner's and enclosed her account for publication in the magazine.

For the next ten years, Wharton brought her imagination to bear on the Italy she loved. The most substantial project was her first full-length novel, *The Valley of Decision* (1902). Composed over a three-year period, the work is a bildungsroman which makes dramatic use of the confused circumstances of the *settecento*. Lewis proposes that this period in Italian history appealed deeply to Wharton as she wearied of Newport's empty rites. "From her American point of view, it seemed to her almost an ideal world: a world of vital interconnectedness, one in which the arts, the play of intellect, the graces of life, and a concern, however laggard, for the betterment of the social order went hand in hand" (58). Although its theme and imagery anticipate the New York novels to follow, *The Valley of Decision* is distinguished by its vivid rendering of this ideal Italian society. Fascinated by Italian palaces and gardens, Wharton next accepted an offer from *Century Magazine* to prepare a book which would be illustrated by Maxfield Parrish. Attempting their first tour by automobile, she and Teddy spent six months of 1903 visiting more than seventy villas and gardens in Italy. The 1904 volume *Italian Villas and Their Gardens* was quickly followed by the 1905 book *Italian Backgrounds*, a personal work capturing what the country meant to her and revealing aspects of the culture neglected by other writers.

A Home in the Berkshires

In America, Wharton was busy creating a home for Teddy and herself outside the boundaries of Newport and New York. She chose the setting of Lenox, Massachusetts in the Berkshires, a different kind of summer community which had been attracting writers and artists since the nineteenth-century sojourns of Nathaniel Hawthorne and Herman Melville. With proceeds from the sale of Land's End, she purchased a property of more than one hundred acres in June 1901 and named it "The Mount" after her great grandfather Ebenezer Stevens' Long Island home. Working closely with architect Francis L. V. Hoppin on renovations, she attempted to apply the European precepts of *The Decoration of Houses* wherever she could. Henry James described the thirty-five room home which resulted as "a delicate French chateau mirrored in a Massachusetts pond . . . and a monument to the almost too impeccable taste of its so accomplished mistress" (*Henry James Letters* 325). The Mount's landscape gardens were another source of pride for Wharton, who devoted considerable energy each summer to gardening (and won seven first prizes in the 1905 Lenox Flower Show). She also savored long visits with her friends in the Berkshires, and she filled her guest rooms with one house party after another.

Visitors to the Mount learned quickly that they would not see their hostess until afternoon, however, for Wharton reserved her mornings for writing. By the time she and Teddy settled into Lenox in the summer of 1904, she was hard at work on the New York novel which she had been considering for several years. In her autobiography, she recounts the difficulties she had in taking up the subject of *The House of Mirth* and giving it moral heft:

In what aspect could a society of irresponsible pleasure-seekers be said to have, on the "old woe of the world," any deeper bearing than the people composing such a society could guess? The answer was that a frivolous society can acquire dramatic significance only through what its frivolity destroys. Its tragic implication lies in its power of debasing people and ideals. The answer, in short, was my heroine, Lily Bart. (*Backward Glance* 207)

In telling the story of her most famous heroine, Wharton discovered that her richest subject was the circumscribed world of her youth. To complete her first novel about Old New York, she formed habits which transformed her "from a drifting amateur into a professional" (*Backward Glance* 209) and enabled her to meet the demanding serial deadlines which she would face for the rest of her life. She was rewarded with success which she had never anticipated, for *The House of Mirth* (1905) was lauded by critics and readers alike. It became the fastest selling book in Scribner's history, and it established her as one of the most important American novelists of the new century.

As Wharton embarked upon the most creative decade of her career, she was beginning a notable friendship with the older writer Henry James. Although she had tried to make his acquaintance as early as 1885, she did not succeed until a December 1903 meeting in London. In the following year, she and Teddy exchanged visits with James, seeing him at Rye in the spring and welcoming him to the Mount in the fall. James was quickly converted to the pleasures of the Whartons' motor car—"a great transformer of life and of the future!"—and he shared her delight in adventures on the road (*Letters of Henry James* 35). The relationship between the writers blossomed quickly, and they remained close friends until his death in 1916. Their sympathy did not extend to each other's literary efforts, however, and she was never his protégé. A strong admirer of *The Portrait of a Lady*, she tried to avoid commenting on his later works and was relieved to note after their first meeting that he spoke more lucidly than he wrote (*Letters* 88).[4] Privately, James regarded her as a popular rather than a serious writer; his biographer Fred Kaplan notes that he found the scale of her wealth and the restless energy of her movements "incompatible with the literary life" (482). Likening himself to "an old croaking barnyard fowl" next to her "golden eagle," James enjoyed portraying Wharton as the Angel of Devastation who wrought havoc in his life whenever she descended with her bristling energy and insatiable appetite for experience (*Letters of Henry James* 125).

La belle époque

Despite their different temperaments, the two friends shared the conviction that European culture was preferable to American culture and chose to spend the most important years of their careers as expatriates. Invigorated by several recent trips to the France of her childhood, Wharton decided at the end of 1906 to take an apartment in Paris rather than spend the winter in New York. The Whartons' luxurious apartment at 53 Rue de Varennes was located in the heart of the Left Bank, among the aristocracy of the Faubourg Saint-Germain. Hoping to negotiate that sophisticated society with the aid of her friend Paul Bourget, Wharton returned to Paris in 1907 to find herself acclaimed as the author of the novel currently appearing in the *Revue de Paris, The House of Mirth*. She comments in her autobiography on the significance of her reception in Paris: "Herein lay one of the many distinctions between the social worlds of New York and Paris. In Paris no one could live without literature, and the fact that I was a professional writer, instead of frightening my fashionable friends, interested them" (*Backward Glance* 261). Wharton took special pleasure in the world of the Parisian salon and the opportunities it afforded her for conversation with writers, artists and academics. She regularly visited Comtesse Rosa de Fitz-James, whose Faubourg salon was the most distinguished in the city during the belle époque. She reveled in the community she found there, for it gave gracious form to the Land of Letters which she regarded as her true home.

Wharton had another reason to settle in the City of Lights, for she was beginning an affair with Morton Fullerton, Paris correspondent for the *London Times*. The two shared a number of interests, and he had visited the Mount in October 1907 at the urging of his mentor Henry James. An urbane companion, he offered her the passion and the sexual fulfillment which she had not experienced in more than twenty years of marriage to Teddy. In daily attendance throughout the winter and spring of 1908, Fullerton inspired more than three hundred love letters and an intimate diary entitled "L'Amê Close" ("The Life Apart"). Their liaison continued through 1909, but he proved to be something less than the soul mate she sought. A sybarite whose history included affairs with both Ronald Gower and Margaret Brooke, he was secretly engaged to his young cousin Katherine throughout his relationship with Wharton and experiencing blackmail at the hands of a different woman. Wharton ended her affair with Fullerton in 1910, though she maintained a friendship with him for years afterward.

Teddy Wharton's health steadily worsened during these turbulent years. Diagnosed with a variety of illnesses since 1902—influenza, gout, neuralgia—he was increasingly prone to depression and intractability by the time he moved with his wife to Paris. Living in the Rue de Varennes made him more unstable, for he remained out of place in the intellectual milieu of the salons and unable to master the French language. With Edith's encouragement, he began to divide his time between resting at the Mount and traveling to various spas in search of cures. Although he found temporary relief from these measures, his condition did not improve. By 1909, it was all too apparent to his doctors that he was suffering from the strain of mental illness which had resulted in the committal and eventual suicide of his father. In the throes of a breakdown that summer, he withdrew fifty thousand dollars from Edith's trust fund and became involved with a young actress in Boston. After arranging for his stay in a Swiss sanitarium—and divesting him of any future role in the management of her accounts—Edith agreed to spend the summer of 1911 with him at the Mount. Her hopes that he would recover in that setting were short-lived, however, and she returned to Paris without him. She never visited the Mount again, but sold it in 1912 and obtained a divorce at the start of 1913.

The strain of Wharton's personal life did not slow her writing. Rather, these were years of impressive productivity, for France provided her with new settings and continuing inspiration. Another example of her lifelong interest in travel, the 1908 work *A Motor-Flight Through France* expresses her sense of the country's varied beauty. Her novels *Madame de Treymes* (1907) and *The Reef* (1912) evoke the inherited traditions and elaborate conventions of the Parisian society which she was observing closely; her satiric masterpiece *The Custom of the Country* (1913) pits its brash heroine Undine Spragg against the rigid hierarchical system of the Faubourg Saint-Germain itself. Although none of these works achieved the success of *The House of Mirth*, Wharton commanded high prices for her writing after 1905 and maintained a wide readership. An account book which she began keeping that year reveals that she earned $125,000 in royalties and serial fees by 1912 (Benstock 261). As Millicent Bell points out, Wharton relied on her pen for most of her adult life: "Though she was born wealthy, she liked to say that she was a self-made woman, for by writing she made much more money than inherited, and she built her literary career like any entrepreneur of non-artistic goods, shrewd and alert in her dealings with her publishers, aware of the market for which she was an industrious producer" (65). A patrician of expansive tastes, Wharton was also a dedicated writer who strove to balance the demands of art and commerce throughout her career.

Ever modest in her remarks on her achievement, Wharton notes in her autobiography that she did not experience the artist's "full control of his implements" until she wrote *Ethan Frome* in 1911 (209). Her thirteenth book in fifteen years, this short novel became her best known and most widely translated work. Although set in the New England environs of the Mount, it began as a French story written during her first year in the Rue de Varennes. Fluent in the French language she had been reading for decades, she began working with a tutor in 1907 to improve her conversational abilities. Accustomed to completing a copy book exercise before each of their sessions, she wrote the short story of a struggling farmer who is trapped in a loveless marriage to an invalid but attracted to another woman. When she returned imaginatively to this situation at the end of 1910, the parallels with her own situation were compelling. R. W. B. Lewis argues that *Ethan Frome* represents a major turning point in Edith's career, precisely because the intense emotion of the fiction reflects the turmoil of its creator. No longer reserving her deepest feelings for her poetry—or venues such as the 1908 "love diary"—she began to express the truth of her inner life in her most representative fiction (308).

Another outlet for Wharton in the years surrounding her divorce was travel with her friends. Visiting New York briefly in late 1913 for the wedding of her niece, she was appalled by the "queer rootless life" she found there and more convinced than ever that she belonged in Europe (*Letters* 312). Estranged from an American society she hardly recognized, she would remain abroad for the next ten years. Following the sale of the Mount, she undertook long trips to Tuscany, Sicily and Spain with Walter Berry. She traveled through Germany with her friend Bernard Berenson and visited Africa with the young writer Percy Lubbock. Temporarily sated by these foreign adventures, she decided in 1914 to lease the country house Stocks in Buckinghamshire (home of Mrs. Humphrey Ward). Wharton looked forward to spending her first summer in England, close to James in Rye.

SERVICE IN THE GREAT WAR

These plans were altered by the June 1914 assassination of the Archduke Franz Ferdinand and the general mobilization of troops which followed. Fiercely committed to the French cause, Wharton soon began the relief work which would define her life for the four years of the Great War. Her first charitable project was the opening of a workroom to aid neighborhood seamstresses who found themselves without the means of supporting their families. Establishing this venture in a large Faubourg apartment with hastily raised funds, she began by paying thirty women to sew clothing needed by area hospitals and other relief organizations. As the number of seamstresses swelled to sixty, she arranged for the sale of the clothes they made and thus created a workroom which remained self-sufficient for the duration of the war.

In the months following the Battle of the Marne, Wharton's humanitarian efforts intensified steadily. As refugees from Belgium and northern France began to pour into Paris, she worked with friends in the fall of 1914 to establish the American Hostels for Refugees. Assisting over nine thousand refugees in their first year of operation, the Hostels did more than provide food, clothing and shelter to the displaced. Under the direction of Wharton and her tireless assistant Elisina Tyler, the Hostels grew to include fourteen dependent organizations supplying help in the form of nurseries, work-rooms, language classes and an employment agency (Benstock 306–07).

At the request of the Belgian government, Wharton founded the Children of Flanders Rescue Committee in April 1915 and opened five houses (on forty-eight hours' notice) to sixty Belgian orphans. This charity would provide housing and supply the needs of nine hundred victims of German bombing, elderly and religious as well as children. Named vice president in 1916 of a French committee attempting to help the growing number of soldiers stricken with tuberculosis in the trenches, Wharton established one additional charity in the form of the "Maisons Americaines de Convalescence" and began opening rest homes for the ill. By 1917, she and Elisina Tyler were overseeing seven sanitoria extending from Paris to Arromanche on the Normandy coast.

Working twelve-hour days for most of the war, Wharton raised enormous sums to sustain these relief organizations operating in twenty-one different houses. She herself raised $82,000 in donations between September 1914 and December 1915; as the war continued, she also depended on an array of American committees working on behalf of "Edith Wharton's War Charities." She had another motive for writing to American readers about wartime conditions, for she was determined to prod the United States into entering the war. Wharton and Walter Berry took four weeklong trips to the front in 1915, always traveling in cars filled to overflowing with food and hospital supplies. The reports of what she saw in the military zone were published in *Scribner's Magazine* and then collected in the book *Fighting France: From Dunkerque to Belfort* (1915). The first American woman to serve as war correspondent, Edith was horrified by the scale of the destruction which she encountered in one village after another and urgent in her efforts as propagandist (Benstock 313). Named Chevalier of the French Legion of Honor early in 1916 in recognition of all her efforts on behalf of the Allies, she was the last civilian so honored during the Great War.

In *A Backward Glance*, Wharton recalls the strong emotions she experienced as she watched the Allied Armies march down the Champs Elysees during the 1919 Victory Parade. "The brief rapture that came with the cessation of war—the blissful thought: 'Now there will be no more killing!'—soon gave way to a growing sense of the waste and loss wrought by those irreparable years. Death and mourning darkened the houses of all my friends, and I mourned with them, and mingled my private grief with the general sorrow" (364). Wharton felt keenly the deaths of Henry James and Egerton Winthrop, and she mourned the wartime sacrifice of a beloved cousin and several younger friends. She had other losses to reckon with as well, for the punishing nature of her charitable work had jeopardized her health. Easily fatigued, she was still recovering from the series of heart attacks which she suffered between May 1917 and June 1918. She was also wrestling with the financial consequences of the war years, when she donated all the money she could spare and never found time for the writing that would replenish her coffers.

Beginning Again in a Changed World

Thus, one of the pressures Wharton faced in the early 1920s was the need to resume the career that had been so profitable. With the notable exception of her New England novel *Summer*, all of her writing during the Great War focused on France and expressed her strong identification with the French people (*The Marne, French Ways and Their Meaning*). Urged by her American editor to write about topics more appropriate for peacetime, she chose the New York society of her youth. Set in the 1870s, *The Age of Innocence* treats Edith Jones's world with an unexpected deference. Acknowledging the unimaginative limits of that New York society, *The Age of Innocence* nonetheless honors the graciousness of a vanished way of life. Increasingly alarmed by the dissonance and confusion of twentieth-century society, Wharton found new meaning in memories of the life she once knew. "When I was young it used to seem to me that the group in which I grew up was like an empty vessel into which no new wine would ever again be poured. Now I see that one of its uses lay in preserving a few drops of an old vintage too rare to be savoured by a youthful palate; and I should like to atone for my unappreciativeness by trying to revive that faint fragrance" (*Backward Glance* 5). Wharton's record of this earlier society found immediate favor with readers and critics alike, for *The Age of Innocence* became a bestseller which earned her $50,000 and the 1921 Pulitzer Prize. The common setting of the later novels *Old New York* (1924), *A Mother's Recompense* (1925) and *The Buccaneers* (1938) reflects her continuing desire to recreate a familiar world.

Another priority for Wharton in the postwar years was arranging a quieter, more satisfying life for herself and her friends. Finding Paris increasingly crowded and shrill, she moved in 1919 to the small village of Saint-Brice-sous-Foret ten miles north of the city. Her first of two new homes was an eighteenth-century house set on seven acres, Pavilion Colombe. After restoring the estate's neglected buildings and gardens in the early 1920s, Wharton spent every spring and fall there. She became a generous patron of the Saint Brice community, hosting village festivals twice a year and a procession on the Feast of the Assumption every August (Dwight 234). Wharton leased a house on the French Riviera for the winter months, returning to the village of Hyères which she had visited during a rare wartime vacation. She purchased Chateau Sainte-Claire in Hyères in 1927 and gathered her closest friends together there every Christmas. Dividing her time between these two courtly homes, she continued the steady entertaining and expert gardening which had enriched her summers at the Mount.

Wharton published regularly through 1937, though she never again enjoyed success on the scale of *The Age of Innocence*. Until the worst years of the Depression, she commanded high fees for her work appearing in popular magazines and relied on this income to support her homes and more than two dozen dependents. Many of the stories and novels which she wrote in the last fifteen years of her life were shaped by her deepening interest in a new subject, the complex relations between parents and children. Wolff suggests that focusing on these relations in novels such as *A Son at the Front* (1923), *Twilight Sleep* (1927) and *The Children* (1928) gave Wharton another way of dramatizing the growing divide which she perceived between past and present. The best of these works also convey the "poignancy of aging" which she was experiencing as her circle of friends shrank and her health began to fail (330–31).

Wharton received numerous awards during these years, so many that Benstock refers to the decade as "the Age of Acclaim" (385). The first woman to receive an honorary degree from Yale University, she returned to the United States one final time in June 1923 to participate in the graduation ceremonies. (Columbia and Rutgers offered her additional degrees in later years, but she was too ill each time to make the voyage and accept the honor.) In 1925, she became the first woman to be awarded a Gold Medal from the National Institute of Arts and Letters for "distinguished services to art or letters in the creation of original work." In 1929, she received a Gold Medal from the American Academy of Arts and Letters for her achievement in fiction and was elected to that prestigious body one year later. Wharton was nominated for the Nobel Prize in 1927 after a group of determined friends campaigned on her behalf. One supporter, Chief Justice William Taft, recommended her nomination on the grounds that she "has reached and sustained a higher level of distinction [in fiction] than that of any other contemporary in her own country" (Lewis 481).

Wharton's steps grew slower as she reached the age of seventy, but she refused to forego several tours of Italy or to curtail her writing. She published *A Backward Glance* in 1933, closing the work with the following appraisal of her circumstances: "Life is the saddest thing there is, next to death; yet there are always new countries to see, new books to read (and I hope to write), a thousand little daily moments when the mere discovery that 'the woodspurge has a cup of three' brings not despair but delight" (379). Increasingly frail after a mild stroke in the spring of 1935, she suffered a more serious stroke in June 1937 and died at the Pavilion Colombe on August 11, 1937. She was buried three days later at Versailles, by the grave of Walter Berry. A band of French war veterans accompanied her casket to the grave, where she was accorded all the honors traditionally reserved for a war hero. In her will, she made generous provision for two of the Maisons de Convalescence which she founded during the Great War.

1

CONTENT

The novel's prologue establishes the narrative structure for the story of Ethan Frome, the scarred figure who arrests the attention of a newcomer to the village of Starkfield, Massachusetts. That curious newcomer serves as Wharton's narrator, described by her in a 1922 introduction to *Ethan Frome* as "the sympathizing intermediary between his rudimentary characters and the more complicated minds to whom he is trying to present them" (Lauer and Wolff xii). A visiting engineer drawn imaginatively to Frome from his first sight of him, the narrator begins the novel by recounting his efforts to learn more about him and the accident which crippled him twenty-four years ago. "I had the story, bit by bit, from various people, and, as generally happens in such cases, each time it was a different story" (63).[1] In these opening words of the novel, the narrator acknowledges the limitations of the story which he received from the village—and anticipates his own version, which will supply the truth of Ethan's experience.

The two representative villagers who offer their different perspectives on the "smash up" are Harmon Gow and Mrs. Hale, and their conversations with the narrator help to frame the novel as a whole. Willing enough to speak about Ethan's terrible sledding accident, the driver Gow manages to inspire more questions than he answers. However, his first remarks about Ethan's predicament are couched in language which directs the narrator's thinking. "'Guess he's been in Starkfield too many winters. Most of the smart ones get away'" (64). Settling into this small village in the Berkshires for a season, the narrator marvels at the frozen world around him and begins to imagine the toll of too many winters there. A lodger in the home of Mrs. Hale, he spends his evenings in her old-fashioned front parlor listening to her anecdotal history of the community. When he raises the subject of Ethan's accident, however, her words slow and she refuses to satisfy his growing curiosity. Endowed with greater sensitivity than Gow, Mrs. Hale will do no more for the narrator than confirm how " 'awful' " the event was (67).

Marked as he is by that awful accident, Ethan is distinguished from his neighbors in other, more important ways. The narrator introduces him as "the most striking figure in Starkfield," finding him a tall and imposing man despite the lameness of his gait and the livid scar on his forehead (63). Watching Ethan's slow progress into the post office for the day's mail, with a halt step suggesting the restriction of a chain, the narrator uses imagery that will deepen in significance as the novel proceeds. It is the "bleak and unapproachable" expression (63) on fifty-two-year-old Ethan's face, however, which drives the visiting engineer to find his own way into the past: "no one gave me an explanation of the look in his face which, as I persisted in thinking, neither poverty nor physical suffering could have put there. Nevertheless, I might have contented myself with the story pieced together from these hints had it not been for the provocation of Mrs. Hale's silence, and—a little later—for the accident of personal contact with the man" (67). Unexpectedly dependent on Ethan for daily transportation to the train midway through his stay, the narrator seeks conversation with his mute driver. Mentioning a job which he completed in Florida the previous year, he is surprised to learn that Ethan visited the state once and hoarded memories of the sunshine for as many winters as he could. Forgetting a book of biochemistry in the buggy one day, the narrator is even more surprised to discover that Ethan took the opportunity to review the science before returning it to him.

Fittingly enough, a winter storm affords the narrator his fullest glimpse of Ethan's hidden life. When heavy snow delays the local train one morning, Ethan offers to undertake the ten-mile drive to the powerhouse in Corbury Junction. On the outskirts of Starkfield, the two men pass the Frome property: an "examinate" sawmill, an orchard of "starved" apple trees, a field buried in snow and "one of those lonely New England farm-houses that make the landscape lonelier" (71). Surveying this isolated scene, the narrator emphasizes the qualities of privation and lifelessness. He reacts strongly to the misshapen home itself, deprived for years of the L-shaped annex traditionally connecting the main house and barn in New England. Sensing regret in Ethan's reference to his father's removal of the "L," the narrator is tempted to identify the mutilated Frome house with the deformed body of its owner. The latter is uncharacteristically talkative as he drives past his home, volunteering that his mother's greatest difficulties began when the railroad " 'side-tracked' " the farm and ended all easy contact between the family and the village (72).

The prologue ends when the narrator enters the Frome farmhouse later that same day. Contending with mounting drifts of snow in the night cold, the two men struggle slowly back from Corbury Junction. When they reach the Frome farm, Ethan indicates that they will travel no further that night and offers shelter to the narrator. As they enter the darkened house together, the narrator immediately registers "a woman's voice droning querulously" behind a closed door (74). In the final gesture recorded in the prologue, Ethan opens this door to the narrator as the droning stops. "It was that night that I found the clue to Ethan Frome, and began to put together this vision of his story" (74). These words are followed by three lines of ellipses, punctuation chosen by Wharton to signify the reader's entrance into the past which is conjured by this famous "vision."

CHAPTER I

The first chapter begins by evoking the conditions of winter which supply the novel with much more than setting. The village of Starkfield is buried under two feet of snow, and the icy stars of Orion and the Dipper hang overhead in a "sky of iron" (75). The only source of light in the empty midnight streets is the basement of the church at the center of town, where a young and vigorous Ethan Frome is walking briskly.

Struck by the stillness and purity of the night air, Ethan finds himself thinking in images drawn from his earlier study of physics. We learn that he attended a technical college in Worcester four or five years earlier and enjoyed experimenting in the laboratory there. Though his father's death led to the end of his studies after only one year, he savors the random associations and images from science which still overtake his thoughts at unexpected moments. The narrator suggests that these studies have animated Ethan's imagination and "made him aware of huge cloudy meanings behind the daily face of things" (76).

Reaching the church at the edge of the village, Ethan pauses a moment before seeking the basement door on the side. In a prominent example of foreshadowing, he considers the quiet hill where his neighbors love to sled throughout the winter. "The pitch of the Corbury road, below lawyer Varnum's spruces, was the favourite coasting-ground of Starkfield, and on clear evenings the church corner rang till late with the shouts of the coasters; but to-night not a sled darkened the whiteness of the long declivity" (76). The only "waking life" in town this night is found within the church, where dance music is playing. Ethan never enters the building but instead positions himself carefully in the shadows by a window. From that dark vantage point, he peers into the brightly lighted hall and watches Denis Eady invite an unidentified young woman to lead the company in one last Virginia reel. In growing turmoil as he watches this dark-haired woman with the red scarf enjoy the dance, he nurses his grievance against the grocer Eady's son and decides that he deserves horse whipping.

The figure who inspires this jealousy is Mattie Silver, a younger cousin of Ethan's wife Zeena. Raised in Stamford, Mattie has been living with the Fromes for the past year and assisting with chores which Zeena is too ill to perform. When Mattie attends the occasional dance or gathering in Starkfield, Ethan walks two miles into town to bring her safely back to the isolated farm. Initially reluctant to assume this responsibility, he now wishes he could spend every evening walking alone with her. Captivated by her since their first meeting at the train, he has found her presence on the farm "like the lighting of a fire on a cold hearth" (78). A figure of vitality and warmth, Mattie is also a kindred spirit who shares Ethan's keen pleasure in the world of nature. Dwelling for years in his own solitary thoughts and impressions, he cherishes every opportunity to "utter his secret soul" to another who responds to the landscape as he does (79).

Watching Mattie laugh and talk with Eady with an easiness he thought reserved for him alone, Ethan begins to brood over her uncertain future in his home. Recognizing that his wife Zeena poses a more immediate threat to that future than Eady, he considers her growing dissatisfaction with Mattie's work. Despite Ethan's efforts to assist Mattie by completing as many of her chores as possible, he knows that she remains unsuited for the housework required of her. He is still shaken by a recent conversation which Zeena began while he was shaving one morning, when she reminded him that she would be needing a "'hired girl'" when Mattie married. Unwilling to concede either as likely—Mattie's marriage or the expense of a hired girl—he claimed that he had no time to discuss the matter further. Zeena's rejoinder about the time which he now spends shaving every morning suggests that she has observed other changes in him as well, but his wife's suspicions have no reality for him as he waits in the dark. "All his life was lived in the sight and sound of Mattie Silver, and he could no longer conceive of its being otherwise" (82). Deeply uneasy as the chapter ends, Ethan remains in the shadows watching Mattie dance with her suitor.

CHAPTER II

The dance has ended and villagers are separating for the night, but Ethan never reveals himself to Mattie when she leaves the church and begins looking for him. A "hidden watcher" fixed in place behind the door, he listens to Eady offer her a ride home and waits tensely for her reply (84). Only after Mattie sets off alone—and refuses Eady a second time—does Ethan join her under the Varnum spruces at the top of the hill. As he attempts clumsily to tease her about the conversation which he has overheard, he delights in her surprise and feels his tension ease "like spring rills in a thaw" (85). Wanting to linger in the dark night with her, he moves closer and loops his arm in hers possessively.

Mattie notes the signs of frequent sledding on the hill before them and comments on the number of people whom she saw coasting earlier in the evening. When Ethan offers to bring her sledding the following night, she accepts with obvious pleasure. She appears to reconsider, however, as she describes the recent accident of two friends on that same hill. She tells him of Ruth Varnum and Ned Hale's near miss with the big elm tree at the bottom, shivering as she remembers how she and other friends thought the pair had died. Ethan is roused to boast that he steers better than Hale, but she insists that the elm tree should be removed altogether.

Unsettled by her manner during this exchange, Ethan seeks reassurance as they near the saw mill on his property. In an effort to probe her feelings, he mentions the last dance of the evening and alludes to village gossip about Eady and her. When Ethan hints that she will be leaving the farm soon, she becomes visibly distressed at the prospect and acknowledges that Zeena is often displeased with her work. " 'You know she hardly ever says anything, and sometimes I can see she ain't suited, and yet I don't know why.' She turned on him with a sudden flash of indignation. 'You'd ought to tell me, Ethan Frome—you'd ought to! Unless *you* want me to go too' " (87). Restored by these words, he savors her closeness once again as she reminds him that she has no other place to go.

As the two draw near the Frome gate, Ethan experiences Mattie's presence as life-giving warmth. With her beside him, even the sight of the family graveyard is pleasing. Accustomed for years to viewing these graves as taunting reminders of his entrapment on the farm, he sees them tonight as signs of continuity. He seeks no changes in his life as long as he has Mattie. " 'I guess we'll never let you go, Matt,' he whispered, as though even the dead, lovers once, must conspire with him to keep her; and brushing by the graves, he thought: 'We'll always go on living here together, and some day she'll lie there beside me' " (88). More language of death follows this ironic foreshadowing, as Ethan and Mattie approach the dark house. Spotting the dead cucumber vine hanging from the porch "like the crape streamer tied to the door for a death," Ethan is tempted to imagine that his wife is not asleep inside but dead (88).

The third member of this household is revealed as the chapter ends. After looking vainly for the house key in its customary place under the mat, Ethan and Mattie are startled when the door is suddenly opened by Zeena herself. Flushed with the pleasure of his hour with Mattie, Ethan is unprepared for the sight of this angular woman swathed in shadows and thinks that he has never seen his wife clearly before. Holding a lamp aloft, Zeena wordlessly ushers Mattie and Ethan into the kitchen, "which had the deadly chill of a vault after the dry cold of the night" (90). Reluctant to accompany Zeena to their bedroom in front of Mattie, he claims that he needs to remain downstairs a while longer to work on mill accounts. As Zeena begins to protest, however, Mattie sends Ethan a warning glance and he reluctantly climbs the stairs to the bedroom which he shares with his wife.

CHAPTER III

Early the next morning, Ethan is tackling his chores against the background of a brilliant winter landscape and musing about the night before, when he fell asleep wondering why he had not kissed Mattie during their walk home. Invigorated by the work at hand, he finds himself reviewing the changes in his home in the year since Mattie's arrival. The first half of the chapter is given over to these reflections, affording Wharton the opportunity to supply exposition and convey the precariousness of Mattie's situation.

Thinking with satisfaction of the ways in which Mattie has blossomed on the farm, Ethan recalls the frail young woman who arrived the previous winter. She was undoubtedly unhappy with the coldness and isolation of her new home, but she never complained to either Ethan or Zeena. Ruefully acknowledging her status as "indentured" to both of them, Ethan considers the losses which Mattie suffered before taking refuge in Starkfield (92). Her father was an ambitious man whose questionable business practices were discovered only after his death, and her mother died soon after learning that she was left with nothing. Alone at the age of twenty, Mattie sold her piano for fifty dollars and began seeking a way to translate her meager skills (trimming hats, making candy, reciting poetry) into gainful employment. Unable to withstand the long hours of work required of her in office or shop, she was soon forced to turn to the unsympathetic relatives ("the clan") who had entrusted their savings to her father (92). Her placement with the Fromes pleased family members intent on payment in some form from Orin Silver and also provided the ailing Zeena with an aide who had no other place to go.

Ethan recalls the first months of Mattie's difficult service, when she could complete few tasks to Zeena's satisfaction and life in the small farmhouse was often tense. Although the greater freedom and ease of summer improved these conditions, he senses a new threat to his peace and lingers over the warning which Mattie tried to communicate to him the previous night. Initially determined to postpone his return to the house, he decides abruptly that he needs to face any trouble directly and heads to breakfast with his hired hand Jotham Powell. When they arrive, Ethan is surprised to find his wife at table dressed for travel. She intends to take the train that day to Bettsbridge, where she will stay overnight with her aunt and consult a new doctor about the symptoms of her illness. Although these sudden journeys invariably require money which Ethan does not have, today he can think of nothing but the fact that he will have a night alone with Mattie.

Lost in happy calculations about the scarcity of winter trains through Corbury Junction, Ethan fails to answer Zeena when she asks if he can spare Jotham to drive her to the station. Even as he belatedly agrees to her request, he is staring unconsciously at Mattie. When he forcibly directs his gaze to Zeena, he sees someone seven years older than he who is already an "old woman": "She sat opposite the window, and the pale light reflected from the banks of snow made her face look more than usually drawn and bloodless, sharpened the three parallel creases between ear and cheek, and drew querulous lines from her thin nose to the corners of her mouth" (95). Loathe to endure a long afternoon's ride with her, he claims that he is unable to take her to the train himself because he needs to collect payment for lumber he is delivering. He regrets the lie immediately, but it appears to have no effect on Zeena.

CHAPTER IV

This chapter begins by sketching the possibilities of a life together for Ethan and Mattie. Their spirits lightened immediately after Zeena's leave-taking, Mattie hums as she works at the sink and Ethan alternately whistles and sings on his way into town. The kitchen itself is renewed in Zeena's absence, appearing "warm and bright" in the winter sunshine (96). Eager to return to it before nightfall, Ethan contemplates how "homelike" it is again without his wife (96). He looks forward to the coming evening, when he and Mattie will share the fire "like a married couple" and experience for the first time the pleasure of being alone together indoors (96).

Encouraged by this prospect, Ethan contemplates moving out of the silence in which he now spends his life. He recalls the conviviality of earlier days in the village and of his year of study with students who treated him with warmth and familiarity. "There was in him a slumbering spark of sociability which the long Starkfield winters had not yet extinguished. By nature grave and inarticulate, he admired recklessness and gaiety in others and was warmed to the marrow by friendly human intercourse" (96). Long deprived of this warmth in his life, he has known only deepening silence since his return to the farm. Forced by his father's accident to assume responsibility for the mill and the farm, he found the loneliness and silence harder to bear than the punishing work itself. His mother's illness left him even more isolated in the house, as she retreated further into herself and refused to speak with him night after night

Reviewing these years of silence—imaged consistently in the novel as a form of imprisonment—Ethan finds his thoughts turning to the cousin who came to nurse his mother at the end. He remembers how grateful he felt toward Zenobia Pierce as she restored order in the household and tended to his mother's needs, all the while filling his home with the human speech which he had been craving. He knows now that he might not have married her if his mother had died in spring rather than winter, for he proposed to Zeena in a moment of "unreasoning dread" that he would be left in silence and isolation once again (97). He entered their marriage confident that they would be leaving the farm as soon as he sold it, for Zeena was accustomed to a busier community than Starkfield and he was inspired by his work in Florida to believe that he could thrive as an engineer in a wider field of action. All of Ethan's hopes for the future collapsed quickly, however, as he searched in vain for a suitable buyer and watched Zeena cultivate the sickliness which has come to define her in Starkfield. The sociability which he sought when he married her ended long ago, returning him to a silent world synonymous in the novel with the season of winter.

Ethan's visit to the village proves no more encouraging than these memories of the past. Delivering his lumber to Andrew Hale, he is rebuffed when he makes the unusual request for payment now rather than three months later. Too proud to press his suit with the kindly builder, he agrees to wait as he and his father have always done. Explaining that he is overextended because of his efforts to complete a house for his son Ned and Ruth Varnum before they marry, Hale jocularly recalls how Ethan was preparing his own home for Zeena " 'not so long ago' " (101). Startled by this public view of his seven years of marriage, Ethan is further discomfited when he spies Denis Eady driving out of town in the direction of the Frome property. Inflamed by jealousy, Ethan passes the church and sees the shadow of a couple embracing under the Varnum spruces. As Ned and Ruth separate guiltily, he contrasts their situation with his own. They can kiss under the trees where he and Mattie stood the night before, for they have no reason to hide their feelings from others.

On his way home to Mattie, Ethan sights a headstone bearing his name in the family graveyard. Fascinated as a child by this stone commemorating an earlier Ethan and his wife of fifty years, he encounters this memento mori now and ponders how quickly his own life (and Zeena's) may pass. Alert for signs that Eady has been visiting, he detects none and whistles his pleasure as he completes his chores in the barn. Encountering a locked door when he reaches the porch, he finds himself waiting in the dark exactly as he did the night before. The woman who admits him this time, however, is not Zeena but a glowing Mattie: "She wore her usual dress of darkish stuff, and there was no bow at her neck; but through her hair she had run a streak of crimson ribbon. This tribute to the unusual transformed and glorified her. She seemed to Ethan taller, fuller, more womanly in shape and motion" (103). Entering the house, Ethan sees that Mattie has taken special pains with their dinner as well. The table is laid with some of his favorite foods, including pickles set out in a conspicuously bright red dish.

Reassured by Mattie that only Jotham Powell has visited in his absence, Ethan begins to enjoy the meal which she has prepared. Yet Zeena seems to intrude on the pair in a variety of ways, and Ethan falters in his efforts at conversation. When Zeena's cat leaps from her chair onto the table, the pickle dish falls to the floor and shatters. Mattie is immediately distraught, explaining to Ethan that the dish was a prized wedding gift from Philadelphia which Zeena never used. Promising to glue the shards of glass together again and return the dish to the top shelf in the china closet, Ethan calms Mattie and directs her to resume their meal together. The "thrilling sense of mastery" which he experiences when she complies reminds him of the control he feels when he is steering a log downhill (106).

CHAPTER V

Ethan and Mattie complete their supper and spend a companionable evening together. Smoking his pipe by the stove while Mattie sews, Ethan thinks with satisfaction that the evening is unfolding exactly as he dreamed it would. "His hard day's work in the keen air made him feel at once lazy and light of mood, and he had a confused sense of being in another world, where all was warmth and harmony and time could bring no change" (107). The two fall into easy conversation about Starkfield acquaintances, and he cultivates the fancy that they have many more evenings like this before them. Remembering their earlier plan to go sledding this moonless evening, they agree that they are perfectly content together where they are.

Yet Ethan is jarred more than once by unwelcome thoughts of his wife. When he persuades Mattie to move to Zeena's chair (where he can see her more clearly) he is unprepared for the result: "As her young brown head detached itself against the patch-work cushion that habitually framed his wife's gaunt countenance, Ethan had a momentary shock. It was almost as if the other face, the face of the superseded woman, had obliterated that of the intruder" (107). Sensing some impediment, Mattie moves quickly back to her own place at the table and resumes her sewing. Zeena becomes the focus of their conversation, however, when Ethan awkwardly tells Mattie that he saw Ruth and Ned kissing under the Varnum spruces. As he moves once again to the subject of Mattie's marriage prospects, she insists on speaking for the first time about Zeena's attitude toward her. The conversation is brief and inconclusive, as neither knows the thoughts of the absent wife.

Increasingly drawn to Mattie, Ethan contents himself with reaching out for the end of the brown cloth which she is sewing. The connection which he experiences is abruptly broken when the cat leaps to catch an unseen mouse and causes a "spectral rocking" of Zeena's empty chair (110). Shaken by this reminder of the wife who will be with them again on the following night, Ethan slowly kisses the fabric which he has been holding. As the clock strikes eleven, the two prepare the house for the night and Ethan provides Mattie with a candlestick before they mount the stairs. Only after she closes her bedroom door does he realize that he has never touched her, "not even her hand" (112).

CHAPTER VI

The chapter opens the following morning at breakfast, when Ethan is filled with such joy that he has difficulty disguising his feelings from Jotham

Powell. Nothing has changed in his wife's absence, but he is suffused with the "sweetness" associated throughout the novel with Mattie, for he now knows the kind of life he might have with her (113). As the two men prepare for the day's work, Ethan is careful to assign Powell the task of bringing Zeena home from the train in the afternoon. He lingers in the kitchen with Mattie after Powell leaves for the barn, acutely conscious that they will not be alone again.

Preoccupied with the need to repair the red pickle dish before Zeena returns from Bettsbridge, Ethan is delayed at every turn during the wet grey morning that follows. Anxious to leave the farm after dinner, he has time only to tell Mattie that he will be home early. Immediately after delivering his lumber he heads to Eady's store, where Denis is unable to produce the bottle of glue which he needs. After further delay at Mrs. Homan's store down the street, he secures the all-important glue. "'I hope Zeena ain't broken anything she sets store by,'" the proprietress calls as Ethan readies his horses for the ride back to the farm (115).

The steady rain which punctuates Ethan's drive home sets the tone for the rest of the chapter. When he rushes from the barn to the kitchen in the belief that Zeena has not yet returned, he finds Mattie alone in the room. She quickly interrupts him as he brandishes the glue bottle, however. After she whispers the news that Zeena is home already, they face each other "pale as culprits" (116). The room in which they stand is already transformed: "He gazed blankly about the kitchen, which looked cold and squalid in the rainy winter twilight" (116). Ethan learns that Mattie can tell him nothing of Zeena's mood, and so heads back to the barn after promising to glue the shattered dish during the night. Powell's repeated refusal to join the family for supper makes Ethan more uneasy, and he returns to his home braced for the news that the Bettsbridge doctor disappointed his wife in some way. He enters to find "the same scene of shining comfort" that greeted him the night before, but he and Mattie await this meal in silence (117).

CHAPTER VII

The first half of this chapter takes place in the Fromes' darkened bedroom, where Ethan reluctantly seeks Zeena at twilight. Still in her traveling clothes, she declines his offer of supper and states that she is sicker than he knows. When she tells him she has been diagnosed with "'complications,'" he is torn between feelings of relief and sympathy (118). (If Zeena has progressed from the undefined "troubles" afflicting so many in Starkfield to "complications," he reasons that she is unlikely to survive very long.) When he encourages her to heed the new doctor's advice, she informs him that she will no longer do any housework but depend instead on a hired girl her aunt has already found for her. In rising temper, Ethan contends that he cannot afford to pay a servant, but Zeena reminds him shrilly that she sacrificed her health to nurse his mother. This first angry exchange of their marriage is likened to "a physical fight between two enemies in the darkness," and he regains control of himself by pausing to light the room's only candle (120).

Attempting to resume their conversation more equably, Ethan promises Zeena that she will be free of all work as the doctor advised. Stung by her taunts about his family's history of poverty, he calmly states that he cannot afford the hired girl from Bettsbridge. He has more difficulty answering her questions about the fifty dollars which he told her he was receiving from Hale, but remains steadfast in his commitment to do all he can for her. Musing aloud about the difficulty, Zeena makes the point that the two will be saving money on Mattie's keep once the new girl arrives. Shocked at the thought of losing Mattie in this way, Ethan tries futilely to remind Zeena that Mattie is a relative deserving of better treatment. " 'She's a pauper that's hung onto us all after her father'd done his best to ruin us. I've kep' her here a whole year. It's somebody else's turn now' " (122). Registering his wife's harsh sentiments, Ethan feels weak and ineffectual. His last effort to intervene on Mattie's behalf leaves him even more shaken and fearful of Zeena's intentions. When he appeals to Zeena to consider what their neighbors might say about this poor treatment of a relative, she answers darkly that she is aware of the gossip already circulating about Mattie's presence in their home.

When Ethan joins Mattie for supper below, she inquires dutifully about Zeena's health and brightens at the prospect of another evening alone with him. Unable to share her gaiety or feign interest in the meal, he soon leaves his seat and takes her in his arms. As she grows more fearful that something is wrong, he loses himself in the pleasure of kissing her and says only that he will not allow her to leave. Her shocked response brings him back to himself, as he realizes that he has made no effort to prepare her for the news which he has just blurted. Rejecting the false hope that "inexorable" Zeena will change her mind, Mattie attempts to reassure Ethan and begins speaking tentatively of finding work again in Stamford (125). Fighting despair, he is vowing to fight Zeena when she unexpectedly enters the kitchen and takes her usual seat for supper. Explaining that she needs to eat in order to preserve her strength, she helps herself to a generous portion of pie and pickles, pets her cat and speaks affably with Mattie about the ailments of various Bettsbridge relatives. Complaining of discomfort at the end of the meal, Zeena leaves the kitchen to find a patent medicine stored in a place which only she knows.

Zeena returns angrily moments later, carrying the jagged fragments of her prized red pickle dish. In the confrontation that follows, she demands to know who is responsible for breaking the dish hidden from view at the top of the china closet. She scorns Ethan's answer that the cat broke the dish, asking how the cat then reassembled the pieces and stored them at the edge of the shelf. When Mattie volunteers that she is to blame for the accident because she wanted to decorate the table, Zeena treats the deed as "sacrilege": " 'You're a bad girl, Mattie Silver, and I always known it.

It's the way your father begun, and I was warned of it when I took you, and I tried to keep my things where you couldn't get at 'em—and now you've took from me the one I cared for most of all' " (128). Overcoming sobs at the close of this speech, Zeena leaves the room cradling the shards of glass as if they were a corpse.

CHAPTER VIII

Ethan and Mattie finish their chores in silence following this confrontation. When he returns from the yard, he finds a note waiting for him in the empty kitchen with the words "Don't trouble, Ethan" (129). Clinging to this slip of paper—the first note he has ever received from Mattie—he retreats to his small, unheated room behind the parlor. In this room which he has modeled on the study of a kindly minister he knew in Worcester, he studies the note and thinks with mounting rebelliousness of his future with Zeena. "Must he wear out all his years at the side of a bitter querulous woman?" (129). Alone in the painfully cold room, he considers how her temperament has soured over the course of their marriage and casts about for a means of escape from her.

The West begins to entice him as the place where he and Mattie can begin their lives apart from Zeena. He recalls the story of another unhappily married young man who prospered in the West after divorcing his wife for the woman he loved. Ethan is comforted by the resolution of this story, thinking of the beautiful golden-haired child who visited New England recently with her happy, successful parents. He also recalls how well the man's first wife fared by selling the farm he left her and beginning a lunch room in Bettsbridge. Inspired by this example, he rises from his makeshift bed and writes the letter which he will leave for Zeena before taking the train with Mattie. Yet as he contemplates leaving Zeena the farm in exchange for his freedom from her, he wonders how he and Mattie will survive in the West without any resources. He is also forced to acknowledge that he will be leaving Zeena without any real assets, given the size of the farm's current mortgage. As he falters, he spies an older newspaper advertising "Trips to the West: Reduced Rates" (131). Reviewing these fares, he realizes that he lacks even the money required to travel West with Mattie. In despair at the prospect of losing her the next day, he sees himself as a "prisoner for life" about to lose the only source of light in his cell (131). When he notes the beautiful moonlit sky outside his window and recalls that he was to take Mattie sledding this night, his misery is complete.

Soon after Ethan wakes to a cold grey dawn, Mattie visits him and confesses that she spent the night listening for the sound of his step on the stair. The two repair to the kitchen, where he is comforted by the familiar rhythms of their morning chores and moved to hope that Zeena will relent and permit Mattie to stay. Seeing Powell on his way to the barn for the morning's work is a predictable sight which encourages Ethan further—until the worker mentions plans already underway for a neighbor to deliver Mattie's large trunk to the station later that day. Ethan rebuffs Powell, claiming that Mattie's departure is not certain. When the men visit the house for breakfast, they find Zeena unusually animated and quick to confirm with Powell that Daniel Byrne will collect Mattie's trunk as planned. The scene in the kitchen ends as Zeena informs Mattie that she will be checking everything packed in the trunk because two small items appear to be missing from the household.

Feeling rebellious and confused in almost equal measure, Ethan heads into Starkfield. Sure that he must act decisively, he has no idea what exactly he should do. Walking through a winter landscape which reminds him again and again of Mattie, he seizes on the idea of pressing Hale (or better yet, his wife) for the fifty dollars he requested earlier. Ethan grows confident that either of the Hales will want to help him when he explains that Zeena is seriously ill and in need of a hired girl. Yet when he faces the kindly Mrs. Hale, he finds himself unable to deceive her in order to secure the money which he needs for his escape West with Mattie. Aware of Ethan's long struggle to support his parents and now his wife, Mrs. Hale expresses genuine concern for him: " 'You've had an awful mean time, Ethan Frome' " (135). Surprised by the sympathy of a neighbor who has always treated him well, he recovers from his "madness" and faces his life honestly (136). Unwilling to desert an ill wife by lying to two friends, he can only make his slow way back to the farm.

CHAPTER IX

This is the longest chapter in the novel, and it brings to a close the narrator's vision of Ethan's life before the "smash up." The opening scene is Mattie's leave-taking from the farm, prepared by the sight of Daniel Byrne waiting by the door for her trunk as Ethan returns wearily from his trip to the village. Finding only Zeena in the kitchen—absorbed in a pamphlet on kidney problems—he rushes to help Mattie bring her heavy trunk downstairs. When he cautiously enters Mattie's room, he notes that she has already stripped it of the small touches which made it cheerful during her stay. She is seated on her trunk in the middle of the room, weeping because she believes she will not see Ethan again. As he holds her close, he hears Zeena calling that Byrne will not wait much longer. Ethan carries the trunk downstairs to the waiting sleigh, feeling as though "his heart was bound with cords which an unseen hand was tightening with every tick of the clock" (138). His only act of defiance follows a dispirited meal, when he insists over Zeena's protests that he will take Mattie to the train himself. He strides to the barn in a temper and soon finds himself repeating the steps he took only a year ago, as he prepared to fetch his wife's cousin home from the train station on the Flats. He drives the sleigh to the house, where he discovers Mattie dressed and waiting in his small room. Zeena is nowhere in sight; she has gone upstairs to rest without saying good-bye to Mattie.

Feeling an unreasoning pleasure as he sets out with Mattie, Ethan brings her to a place associated with one of their fondest summer memories. As they drive around Shadow Pond, he reflects on the way it embodies feelings which he cannot articulate: "It was a shy secret spot, full of the same dark melancholy that Ethan felt in his heart" (141). Alighting by a small beach, they sit together on the same fallen tree where they visited during a church picnic the previous summer. He recalls arriving unexpectedly at the end of his day's work, finding Mattie among her friends "bright as a blackberry under her spreading hat" (142). Eager to greet him, she left the festivities to bring him coffee and spend a few moments alone with him on this tree trunk. Lulled by the warmth of these memories from a special day, Ethan indulges in the dream that he is a single man courting the woman whom he hopes to marry. Mattie soon insists that they return to the sleigh, however, and the sun sets as they leave Shadow Pond.

The ride to town is filled with words and feelings which Ethan is finally able to express. He asks Mattie's plans for the future and protests that she is not strong enough to resume long hours on her feet in a Stamford store. Learning that she has no other relatives willing to help her, he makes his frustrated desires clear: " 'You know there's nothing I wouldn't do for you if I could' " (143). As he tells her that he would leave with her if he were free, she produces the letter which he began writing to Zeena the night before. In response to his urgent questions, Mattie tears the letter in pieces but confesses that she has been filled with similar thoughts and desires since the picnic at Shadow Pond. Both are silent as they near the village, making their descent in darkness which is "dropping down like a black veil from the heavy hemlock boughs" (144). Within this darkness, Ethan reiterates his helplessness (" 'I'm tied hand and foot, Matt' ") and glumly raises the prospect of Mattie's marriage to another (144). She rejects this possibility in a flood of tears, telling him that she would rather die than leave him.

As Ethan and Mattie approach the lights of the village, they observe children sledding by the church where they had intended to coast. He impulsively insists that he will take her down the hill before she leaves Starkfield and refuses to consider the hired girl waiting for him at the Flats. Finding a suitable sled, he assures Mattie that he is adept at navigating in the darkness which surrounds them (though he hesitates briefly as they begin their descent). They are exhilarated by the speed of the ride, despite the big elm which they pass in their flight. As they slowly mount the silent hill afterward, he is stricken with the thought that they will not walk together again. Passing under the Varnum spruces, Mattie asks where Ruth and Ned kissed the previous day and draws Ethan to her for a final embrace. As the clock strikes five, they cling to each other more fiercely and he speaks their refusal to be separated: " 'What's the good of either of us going anywheres without the other one now?' " (147). Mattie's response is swift, for she wants Ethan to prevent their separation by steering them down the hill directly into the big elm.

Mattie advances this proposal in conditions of unrelieved darkness and silence, for villagers have abandoned the streets below for their evening meal. Treated by the narrator as an "embodied instrument of fate," she goads Ethan to consider the sterile life that he will be resuming at the farm without her (148). Initially resistant to the idea of suicide, he is moved by the blackness around them to imagine that they are already in their graves. Distracted by the hungry whinnying of his sorrel, he offers no resistance when Mattie pulls him toward the sled. He attempts to assume control over events by seating her behind him this time, however. Nearly bolting from the sled at the last moment, he reminds himself that death is better than parting and sets off down the steep hill. Startled by the sudden, unwelcome image of his wife's face, he flinches as they near the elm and rights the sled with difficulty. The crash which occurs next is suggested by a disruption of the prose, followed by Ethan's slow return to consciousness. Trapped by a massive weight which he cannot identity, he gradually becomes aware of a small animal nearby crying in such pain that he feels it in his own body. He locates the source of the sound in Mattie, who wakes with difficulty and says his name. Ethan laments their defeat with the words, " 'Oh, Matt, I thought we'd fetched it,' " as his sorral whinnies again from the world which they have tried to flee (151). The chapter ends with three lines of ellipses signifying our return to the present day.

Entering the Frome kitchen, the narrator registers a "querulous drone" which stops so quickly that he cannot identify who has been speaking (152). He finds two women seated in the cold room, sallow and gaunt figures distinguished chiefly by height. The woman who rises indifferently to prepare the evening meal is Zeena; the woman with the "bright witch-like stare" is Mattie (152). The stark poverty of their surroundings strikes the narrator forcefully, and the brief interlude ends as Ethan awkwardly introduces his wife and her cousin to him.

The remainder of this epilogue occurs in the more familiar setting of Mrs. Hale's front parlor, where the narrator completes his imaginative reconstruction of Ethan's past. Relieved that both men survived their trip during the greatest blizzard of the winter, Mrs. Hale and her mother (Mrs. Varnum) are openly curious about the narrator's overnight stay at the farm. By the women's reckoning, he is the first stranger to enter that bleak household in more than twenty years. Mrs. Hale recalls going to the farm often in the months following the accident—along with other concerned neighbors—until she began to sense that the Fromes craved solitude more than assistance. She now confines her visits to two a year, explaining that she tries to spare Ethan's pride by stopping in when he is elsewhere: " 'It's bad enough to see the two women sitting there—but *his* face, when he looks round that bare place, just kills me.... You see, I can look back and call it up in his mother's day, before their troubles' " (154). The narrator recalls the sight of Ethan,

Zeena and Mattie close together in the barren room and murmurs his ready assent.

Alone with her lodger after her mother retires, Mrs. Hale begins sharing memories which she has guarded for twenty-four years. She speaks without preamble of the evening the accident occurred, remembering how she kept watch through the long night after Mattie Silver was brought to her house. She falls silent as she recounts what happened when the injured woman woke up briefly and spoke to her, for even now she cannot bring herself to repeat Mattie's words of pain. This kindly villager resumes her narrative by describing Zeena nursing Ethan selflessly at the minister's house, while the village gossiped about the news that Mattie had been sent away peremptorily and speculated about her ride down the hill with her cousin's husband. Emphasizing the sacrifices required of all three in the years since the accident, Mrs. Hale adds that Ethan's burden remains the heaviest—for he is the unwilling witness of the terrible quarrels between the two women forced to live together. Removing her glasses in a gesture promising greater frankness still, she tells of the day soon after the accident when it appeared that her friend Mattie would die. Repeating the words she spoke years ago, Mrs. Hale insists that it would have been better for all if Mattie had died: " 'And I say, if she'd ha' died, Ethan might ha' lived; and the way they are now, I don't see's there's much difference between the Fromes up at the farm and the Fromes down in the graveyard; 'cept that down there they're all quiet, and the women have got to hold their tongues' " (150). The novel ends with this somber appraisal of Ethan's fate.

2

---·•◆•·---

TEXTS

The publication of *Ethan Frome* was a singular event in Edith Wharton's long career. The novel ran in *Scribner's Magazine* from August through October 1911, and it appeared in book form at the end of September that same year. It has since become the best known and most widely read of all Wharton's fiction, despite the fact that it is set in an isolated farmhouse in western Massachusetts rather than a brownstone in Old New York. To evoke a world completely different from the cosmopolitan milieu of her society novels, Wharton drew on impressions of New England village life formed during her summers in residence at the Mount in Lenox, Massachusetts (1902–1911). Those impressions of life in the Berkshires resulted in two powerful works, *Ethan Frome* and the later *Summer* (1917), which challenge the accuracy of late nineteenth-century portrayals of New England. Wharton's efforts to depict the harshness of Ethan Frome's life in the fictional Starkfield imbued her with new confidence in her powers as an artist, for she took special pleasure in the writing of the novel and unaccustomed pride in the finished work. Acknowledging favorable reviews which the novel received, she crowed in a 1911 letter to Morton Fullerton, "They don't know *why* it's good, but they are right: it *is*" (*Letters* 260–61). Savoring her newfound control over fictional form and language, Wharton regarded the publication of *Ethan Frome* as the end of her long apprenticeship as a writer (Wolff 58).

BACKGROUND

A tragic sledding accident which occurred in Lenox is commonly regarded as Wharton's inspiration for the climax of *Ethan Frome*.[1] Five young friends were completing a series of runs down the mile-long slope of Courthouse Hill shortly after 4:00 p.m. on March 11, 1904. The coasting party consisted of four young women and one young man, all of them eighteen years old and all but one members of the junior class at Lenox High School. According to the *Berkshire Evening Eagle*, Hazel Crosby was trying her hand at steering the large sled known as a "double ripper" as it raced down the long hill at the speed of fifty miles per hour. She apparently lost control of the sled after hitting an icy rut and crashed into a gas light pole at the foot of the hill. All five young people were thrown from the sled onto the ice, and Hazel Crosby died that same evening of multiple fractures and internal injuries. One of the passengers was lamed by the accident, and two others were permanently scarred (Lewis 308). The timing of this late afternoon accident at the end of winter is repeated in the novel—involving a slope named School House Hill rather than Courthouse Hill—leaving Ethan and Mattie similarly scarred and crippled after their "smash up" (63).

Wharton was abroad in the winter of 1904, but she undoubtedly learned of the March accident when she returned to the Mount that summer. The resort community of Lenox was only one of the Berkshire villages which would appear under a different name in *Ethan Frome*; others which the writer knew from her visits to the Nortons in Ashfield (Plainfield and Stockbridge, for example) would become Bettsbridge, Corbury Flats and Corbury Junction in the novel (Lewis 309). Scott Marshall points to an even more compelling connection between the 1904 accident and the 1911 novel: "What has not been generally known is that Wharton was personally acquainted with one of the injured victims of the 1904 accident, Kate Spencer, and that their friendship developed during the period when *Ethan Frome* was conceived and written" ("Wharton, Spencer" 20). As associate manager of the local library (a volunteer position which she held as long as she owned the Mount), Wharton worked regularly with Assistant Librarian Kate Spencer. When the latter was forced to resign her position in 1909 for health reasons, the writer expressed her regret in a letter from England and continued to send the young woman Christmas gifts. The importance of this association for Wharton becomes all the more apparent when one considers the injuries which Spencer suffered in the accident, a dislocated right hip and a permanently scarred face. Their influence on the creation of Wharton's title character seems clear, for he is marked by a "red gash" across his forehead and a "shortened and warped" right side (63).

AN EARLY VERSION

The novel is rooted in the frozen winter landscape of New England, but it began as a French exercise designed to strengthen Wharton's command of the language. Although she never acknowledged her use of the 1904 sledding accident in Lenox, she commented freely on the circumstances surrounding her first attempt to tell Ethan Frome's story. She writes in her autobiography *A Backward Glance*, "I have a clearer recollection of its beginnings than of those of my other tales, through the singular accident that its first pages were written—in French!" (295). Settling happily into Paris for the first of many seasons there, Wharton was spurred by a friend's teasing to seek help with her conversational French in the winter of 1907. Having learned the language in her childhood, she found few opportunities to speak it in adulthood and maintained her fluency by reading favorite authors such as Racine and Corneille. Told by a French friend that she was speaking in the writers' seventeenth-century idioms ("the purest Louis Quatorze"), she sought a tutor who would help her:

An amiable young man was found; but, being too amiable ever to correct my spoken mistakes, he finally hit on the expedient of asking me to prepare an "exercise" before each visit. The easiest thing for me was to write a story; and thus the French version of "Ethan Frome" was begun, and carried on for a few weeks. Then the lessons were given up, and the copy-book containing my "exercise" vanished forever. (295)

The original black notebook containing this early effort was not lost, fortunately, and is available in the Beinecke Library at Yale. A scant eight pages long, this preliminary sketch introduces the three figures of the novel and identifies the circumstances in which they are trapped.[2]

In this untitled story, Hart (Ethan) is a struggling farmer married to a difficult, sickly woman named Anna (Zeena). He has fallen in love with her younger cousin Mattie, who lives with them and helps with chores. The story opens as Hart and Mattie are walking together outdoors, speaking urgently about the fact that she is being sent away by his suspicious wife. Anna soon leaves for an overnight trip to see a doctor in a neighboring town, but Hart spends the evening in the village tavern rather than alone in the house with Mattie. Upon her return, Anna unveils plans for Mattie to work in a distant city. Hart wants to defy his wife, but Mattie insists on going because Anna is the only relative who has been kind to her. The story ends as Mattie and Hart take their leave of one another at the train. Tallying the many differences between Wharton's two versions of this story, Cynthia Griffin Wolff comments, "What we have in the Black Book *Ethan* is only the germ of an idea—a lengthy donnée that has not yet been explored and shaped and wrought into a focused fiction" (158). The sledding accident which forms the climax of the novel is conspicuously absent, as is the narrative structure which is so important to Wharton's presentation of Ethan.

THE NARRATIVE STRUCTURE

Wharton wrote generously about the composition of *Ethan Frome* for years after its publication, in prefaces and essays as well as in her autobiography.

This willingness to write about a finished work is another measure of the novel's importance to her, for throughout her long career she reserved comments on her fiction for private correspondence with close friends. Her introduction to the 1922 Modern Student's Library edition of the novel was the first which she ever agreed to supply for a work of her own, and it was followed years later by a preface to the 1936 dramatization of *Ethan Frome* by Owen and Donald Davis.[3] When she learned in 1926 that Scribner's was planning a new edition of the novel for the Modern Student's Library series, to be issued with a different introduction, she reacted swiftly:

I should be very glad to have it appear in this series, and the royalty suggested is perfectly satisfactory in the circumstances; but I should like, without appearing indiscreet, to ask about the proposed author of the introduction.

I am rather fond of "Ethan Frome," and I should not care to have it spoken of by any one who does not understand what I was trying to do. Would you mind telling me a little about Professor Erskine's capacity for writing of the technique of fiction? How I wish that Mr. Brownell would do this preface for me! Is it quite impossible to persuade him to? (Wolff 155–56)

The protectiveness which Wharton expresses here reflects more than her oft-quoted regard for *Ethan Frome* as the first proof of her coming of age as an artist. Her concern over the new introduction (eventually abandoned altogether by Scribner's) is rooted even more firmly in her continuing interest in the design of the novel, specifically in the "technique" which she employed.

Not surprisingly then, Wharton's various commentaries on *Ethan Frome* are devoted to two broad concerns. Mindful of all who assumed that a patrician of Old New York knew nothing of impoverished Berkshire villages, she strove to establish her thorough familiarity with the New England "hill-people" of frozen Starkfield (*Backward Glance* 296). She took even greater pains with the narrative structure of the novel, for it was the chief source of her pride in the finished work. Her 1922 introduction provides her fullest analysis of the problems which she faced in attempting to tell the story of figures whom she describes as "*granite outcroppings*, but half-emerged from the soil, and scarcely more articulate" (xi). She recalls wondering how to render the austerity of their experience without falsifying it, especially within the complicated time frame of the narrative. She presents her answer in the form of her "scheme of construction," the narrative structure allowing her to set a sophisticated observer (a "looker-on") among simple people unable or unwilling to narrate Ethan Frome's life (xii). "Each of my chroniclers contributes to the narrative *just so much as he or she is capable of understanding* of what, to them, is a complicated and mysterious case; and only the narrator of the tale has scope enough to see it all, to resolve it back into simplicity, and to put it in its rightful place among his larger categories" (xiii). The limitations of the accounts which the narrator gathers are intentional, for Wharton chose the narrative method which would accommodate a variety of perspectives on the action of the novel.

Wharton emphasizes in the 1922 introduction that she was hardly the first to incorporate multiple viewpoints into her fiction. Acknowledging her debt to two writers in particular, she cites the "magnificent example" of the earlier works "La Grande Breteche" by Honore Balzac (1842) and *The Ring and the Book* by Robert Browning (1868–1869). The Balzac story appears in a collection entitled *Another View of Woman*, itself part of the writer's vast masterpiece *The Human Comedy*. The narrator of "La Grande Breteche" is Dr. Bianchon, one of several dinner guests telling stories late into the night. Taking his turn after 2:00 a.m., the doctor describes an empty, ruined mansion which he once encountered on a visit to Brittany. Accustomed to visiting its neglected gardens in the evening, he returned to his inn one night to discover a local notary waiting to speak with him.

Executor of the curious will written by the deceased owner of La Grande Breteche, Monsieur Regnault is the first of three townspeople to speak with Dr. Bianchon about the mysterious events which occurred there. Regnault concentrates on the lonely ends of Monsieur and Madame de Merret and on the provision in her will stipulating that no one enter their home again after her death. The doctor's second visitor, innkeeper Madame Lepas, supplies the history of a Spanish aristocrat who was imprisoned for a time in the inn. A devout man with a distinctive ebony and ivory crucifix, he attended Mass often and always positioned himself close to Madame de Merret's chapel within the church. The remainder of the storytelling falls to Rosalie, a servant who was present on the night that Monsieur de Merret returned home unexpectedly and grew suspicious that his wife was hiding someone in her closet. After Madame de Merret swore solemnly—on an ebony and ivory crucifix—that no one was inside the closet, her husband ordered a mason to wall in the door. Rosalie concludes by reporting that Monsieur de Merret then remained in his wife's room for the next twenty days, reminding Madame de Merret when she attempted to speak on behalf of the dying figure in the closet that she had sworn that no one was there. Dr. Bianchon makes no comment on this last account, and "La Grande Breteche" ends as all the women at table rise and leave wordlessly.

The second influence which Wharton cites features another jealous spouse driven to violence, as well as even more sophisticated control of multiple perspectives on a central action. Robert Browning's epic poem *The Ring and the Book* focuses on a 1698 triple murder which occurred in Rome, and his famous source is the Old Yellow Book which he found in a Florence flea market in June 1860. The story centers on the trial of Count Guido Franceschini, accused of savagely murdering his young wife Pompilia and her parents after learning of the birth of her son. Increasingly unhappy and mistreated since her 1693 marriage to Guido, Pompilia had escaped from his home in Arezzo eight months earlier with the help of the young priest Giuseppe Caponsacchi. Captured by Guido at an inn en route to her parents in Rome, the wife and the cleric were sentenced for the crimes of flight and adultery. Released when her pregnancy was discovered, Pompilia returned to her parents' home to await the birth of her child. She died four days after the murderous attack by her husband and his henchman.

The twelve books which comprise Browning's epic consist of dramatic monologues from a range of observers absorbed in Guido's trial for these crimes. Browning himself begins and ends the work, and all but one of the volumes in between are divided among three different sets of voices: gossips in the streets of Rome, the central figures themselves (Guido, Pompilia, Caponsacchi) and lawyers arguing the merits of their cases. Through these colorful narratives, *The Ring and the Book* explores a series of unifying questions concerning a husband's rights, a wife's innocence and the nature of truth itself. Dramatizing the ambiguity of so many human perspectives, the epic ends with the poet's meditation on the unique power of art to reach truth:

> This lesson, that our human speech is naught,
> Our human testimony false, our fame
> And human estimation words and wind.
> Why take the artistic way to prove so much?
> Because, it is the glory and good of Art,
> That Art remains the one way possible
> Of speaking truth, to mouths like mine, at least. (ll. 834–40)

In testing the limits of the individual observer's ability to convey truth, the superb poetry of *The Ring and the Book* reveals the irony informing narrative structure in so many works of modern fiction. The uncertain "human testimony" which Wharton found in Balzac's story and Browning's monologues inspired her to experiment with point of view when she began writing her novel.

THE "SMASH UP" IN WHARTON'S LIFE AND FICTION

In her autobiography, Wharton maintains that it was the unexpected sight of Bear Mountain in the Berkshires which reminded her of Hart's story and inspired her to write *Ethan Frome*. Important as setting is to both of Wharton's New England novels, her biography supplies other, more compelling reasons for her renewed interest in this trapped farmer at the end of 1910. *Ethan Frome* was the first novel which Wharton completed following 1907's *The Fruit of the Tree*; in the four years intervening, she published the story collection *The Wild Woman and the Hermit* (1908) and concentrated on the poetry which appeared in the volume *Artemis to Actaeon* (1909). She also made several starts at her comic masterpiece *The Custom of the Country* during these years, but the turbulence of this period in her life (and her resulting bouts of ill health) meant that she was forced to put this manuscript aside more than once and to postpone indefinitely its serialization in *Scribner's Magazine*. Coping with the needs of an increasingly unstable husband, she had few opportunities to write fiction as the decade drew to a close.

When Wharton was able to resume her daily writing in 1910, she turned to *Ethan Frome* and not *The Custom of the Country*. Choosing to tell the darker of these two stories allowed her to express the entrapment which she felt in her marriage to Teddy—and the liberation which she had experienced in her recent affair with W. Morton Fullerton. The influence of Wharton's private life on the novel which resulted is widely acknowledged by her biographers and critics, who pay special attention to the course of her tumultuous affair with Fullerton and the "overwrought emotionalism" of the years immediately preceding the writing of *Ethan Frome* (Murad 90). Kenneth M. Price and Phyllis McBride comment, "The relationship developed as Wharton was entering her greatest phase as a writer, and the affair had a significant impact on her fiction and a profound impact on her life" (664). The intensity of new emotions which she experienced from the start of this relationship in late 1907 to its end in 1910 inspired the tone and texture of *Ethan Frome*. The doubts which racked her when she was separated from the enigmatic Fullerton found their form in the doomed romance itself. Even the "smash up" of Ethan and Mattie on Courthouse Hill, absent from the 1907 version, is anticipated in the striking imagery which Wharton used in a 1908 letter to the absent Fullerton:

This is one of the days when it is more than I can bear.—
I suppose I ought to qualify that more by an "almost," since I am here & the lake is là-bas—& I *am* bearing it. But just now, when I heard that the motor, en route for Havre, had run into a tree and been smashed (bursting tire), I felt the wish that I had been in it, & smashed with it, & nothing left of all this disquiet but a "coeur arrête." (*Letters* 147)

Stranded at the Mount for the summer of 1908 without benefit of Fullerton's company, Wharton imagined the release of death available through the act of crashing into a tree. Her biographer Eleanor Dwight suggests that the violent sentiment of this letter, bred of Wharton's desperate loneliness apart from Fullerton, influenced the novel as powerfully as the 1904 sledding accident in Lenox (171–72).

A short story which Wharton completed in that same month offers additional insight into the strong emotions governing her imagination in this period. Accustomed to the pleasure of regular meetings with Fullerton in Paris throughout the winter and spring of 1908, she returned to America most reluctantly in June. She composed the short story "The Choice" in a single sitting on her fifth day of sailing, in what Lewis calls "a burst of savagery and despair" (228). At the center of this work is Isabella Stilling, a woman of Wharton's age and refinement who is unhappily married to the garrulous Cobham and romantically involved with their friend Austin Wrayford. Her dilemma is captured in the opening scene, as she observes Cobham play the squire in an imposing home suggestive of the Mount: "No one else within a radius of a hundred miles (on a conservative estimate) had as many horses, as many greenhouses, as many servants, and assuredly no one else had two motors, or a motor-boat for the lake" (1). A sports enthusiast dependent on his wife's trust fund for the comforts he enjoys, Cobham bears a striking resemblance to Teddy Wharton (Lewis 228). (Wharton invites other comparisons between her character Stilling and her husband, including their ease in company and their sentimental devotion to their mothers.) On the night on which the story takes place, Stilling acknowledges to Wrayford that he has squandered more of his wife's funds on Wall Street and requires her signature on a note. Ironically, Stilling asks Wrayford to inform Isabella of these setbacks and secure her agreement to the loan.

The title of "The Choice" refers to an even more serious decision which Isabella must make, however. The work's climax occurs in the boathouse on the Stilling property, where she and Wrayford have been meeting secretly. Pressed by him to leave her husband, she confesses the intensity of her desire for Stilling's death in the sharpest outburst of the story:

Sometimes? I wish it always—every day, every hour, every moment! . . .
I'm not the saint you suppose; the duty I do is poisoned by the thoughts I think. Day by day, hour by hour, I wish him dead. When he goes out I pray for something to happen; when he comes back I say to myself: "Are you here again?" When I hear of people being killed in accidents I think: "Why wasn't he there?" When I read the death-notices in the paper I say: "So-and-so was just his age." When I see him taking such care of his health and diet,—as he does, you know, except when he gets reckless and begins to drink too much,—when I see him exercising and resting, and eating only certain things, and weighing himself, and feeling his muscles, and boasting that he hasn't gained a pound, I think of the men who die from overwork, who throw their lives away for some big object, and I say to myself: "What can kill a man who thinks only of himself?" And night after night I keep myself from going to sleep for fear I may dream that he's dead. When I dream that, and wake and find him there, it's worse than ever—and my thoughts are worse than ever, too! (38)

Isabella's ardent desire for her husband's death suggests the depth of Wharton's need for Fullerton rather than Teddy, of course, but it also anticipates an important strain of feeling in the later work *Ethan Frome*. Desperate for a life with Mattie, Ethan imagines the death of Zeena on more than one occasion: he fantasizes at the close of Chapter II that tramps have killed his wife, and he struggles to respond sympathetically in Chapter VII when Zeena tells him she has been diagnosed with ominous-sounding "complications" (118). Neither Isabella nor Ethan is granted this dark wish of a spouse's death, however, and Wharton herself remained with Teddy until 1911. At the end of "The Choice" a drunken Stilling startles his wife and her lover by entering the boathouse to check his new launch, and both men are soon plunged into the water below the sliding floor. Struggling to help Wrayford to safety, Isabella rescues Stilling instead—and thus forfeits her choice.

Wharton did not include this story in her 1908 collection *The Wild Woman and the Hermit* (though she did publish it in *Century Magazine*). Her biographer Wolff points out that "The Choice" lacks the control of Wharton's more accomplished fiction and suggests that her experience with Fullerton was still too recent to be transformed into art (148). Another narrative which Wharton attempted in this turbulent period was never published in her lifetime, though its language and imagery resonate through-out *Ethan Frome*. Known as the "Love Diary," it records Wharton's thoughts and feelings as she began her relationship with Fullerton and is addressed to him.[4] The journal spans seven months in Wharton's life, starting three days after Fullerton's first visit to the Mount in October 1907 and ending as she was leaving Paris in June 1908. The writer named this private diary "The Life Apart (L'amê close)," drawing the French phrase for "the enclosed soul" from a sixteenth-century love poem by Pierre Ronsard: "Une tristesse dans l'amê close/Me nourrit, et non autre chose ["A sadness in my shut-in soul/Nourishes me, and no other thing"] (Lewis 191–92). Wharton chose these poignant lines as epigraph for the Love Diary, and they help to establish a theme which she develops throughout the reflections and literary quotations which follow. Lewis comments that Wharton ima-gined herself in the years before her affair with Fullerton as "gazing out through the bars of a prison at the procession of life" (192). Intended as more than the private musings of a woman in love, the journal is a literary effort which begins by establishing the condition of the author as someone long accustomed to "the emotional imprisonment" of her marriage (Price and McBride 669).

This motif of the Love Diary, developed from the epigraph to the closing entries, is a prominent feature of *Ethan Frome* as well. Throughout the Love Diary, Wharton expresses her need for release from the life in which she has been trapped since her marriage to Teddy. Late in the work—in an entry written after her crossing to America—she presents Fullerton with an episode which is meant to convey the impossibility of her life with Teddy:

In the train yesterday I was reading Lock's Heredity & Variation, & struck by a curious & rather amusing passage, held it out & said: "Read that."
    The answer was: "Does that sort of thing really amuse you?"—I heard the key turn in my prison-lock.—That is the answer to everything worth while! . . .

And yet I must be just. I have stood it all these years, & hardly felt it, because I had created a world of my own, in which I lived without heeding what went on outside. But since I have known what it was to have some one enter into that world & live there with me, the mortal solitude I came back to has become terrible. (Price and McBride 662)

The metaphor of the key turning in the lock conveys vividly Wharton's sense of her own captivity, all the more pronounced now after her experience of union with another. When she returned to novel writing after the close of her affair, she drew on this imagery for her characterization of the lonely farmer Ethan. On the first page of the novel, the narrator renders the halting quality of Ethan's gait as "a lameness checking each step like the jerk of a chain" (63). When Ethan is forced to acknowledge in Chapter VIII that he cannot escape to the West with Mattie, he imagines himself as confined for the rest of his life: "The inexorable facts closed in on him like prison-warders hand-cuffing a convict. There was no way out—none. He was a prisoner for life, and now his one ray of light was to be extinguished" (131). Like his creator, he feels his "mortal solitude" all the more keenly for having found someone capable of releasing him from his prison cell.

Morton Fullerton is characterized in the Love Diary by his appreciation for beauty, a trait which helps him to liberate the lonely Wharton. In an April entry, she exults over the discovery of another with whom she can share long suppressed sentiments: "It is curious how the scraps of verse I wrote from time to time in the past, when a wave of Beauty rushed over me, & I felt *I must tell some one!*—it is curious how they express what I am feeling now, how they say more than I then understood, & how they go straight to you, like homing birds released long long ago by a hand that knew not whence they came!" (Price and McBride 675). The language of flight conveys the writer's sense of freedom in the company of one who responds to the beauty of art as she does. The Love Diary celebrates this aspect of her relationship with Fullerton, all the more emphatically as she prepares to leave him in the spring.

How often I used to say to myself: "No one can love life as I do, love the beauty & the splendour & the ardour, & find words for them as I can, without having a share in them some day"—I mean the dear intimate share that one guessed at, always, beyond & behind their universal thrill!—And the day came—the day has *been*—& I have poured into it all my stored-up joy of living, all my sense of the beauty & mystery of the world, every impression of joy & loveliness, in sight or sound or touch, that I ever figured to myself in all the lovely days when I used to weave such sensations into a veil of colour to hide the great blank behind. (Price and McBride 680)

These grateful words from the Love Diary echo unexpectedly in *Ethan Frome*, for Wharton's taciturn farmer also loves the beauty of the natural world around him. Like the writer of "The Life Apart," he feels joy when his long-standing isolation is penetrated by a responsive soul:

He had always been more sensitive than the people about him to the appeal of natural beauty. His unfinished studies had given form to this sensibility and even in his unhappiest moments field and sky spoke to him with a deep and powerful persuasion. But hitherto the emotion had remained in him as a silent ache, veiling with sadness the beauty that evoked it. He did not even know whether any one else in the world felt as he did, or whether he was the sole victim of this mournful privilege. Then he learned that one other spirit had trembled with the same touch of wonder: that at his side, living under his roof and eating his bread, was a creature to whom he could say: "That's Orion down yonder." (79)

For Ethan, this heightened awareness of the beauty around him is "mournful privilege" merely deepening his loneliness before he meets Mattie. When he finds her responding with the same joy and wonder to the sights he treasures, however, he is freed from his silence. She alone possesses the language to express what he thinks of as his "secret soul" (79).

There are other lines of continuity between the Love Diary and the novel *Ethan Frome*, for each work explores the intensity of love and desire in a figure deprived of both. Certain images found in the private journal prepare the more developed patterns of the later fiction, including Wharton's use of cold and ice to describe her state before she knew Fullerton. "I have been warmed through & through, never to grow quite cold again till the end," she writes triumphantly in the May 21st entry (Price and McBride 680). Such language permeates the 1911 novel, for Ethan experiences Mattie again and again as a source of warmth (as well as light) in his frozen world. For him, her arrival means "the lighting of a fire on a cold hearth" (78), and her growing closeness brings with it the heat of spring and even summer. Her presence on the occasion of Zeena's overnight visit to Bettsbridge transforms the Frome kitchen into a place that is suddenly "warm and bright" again, and he finds himself fantasizing about an unbroken string of evenings by the fire with Mattie: "For the first time they would be alone together indoors, and they would sit there, one on each side of the stove, like a married couple, he in his stocking feet and smoking his pipe, she laughing and talking in that funny way she had, which was always as new to him as if he had never heard her before" (96). This dream of Ethan's originates in the earlier Love Diary, most clearly in the February 21st entry where Wharton indulges in the happy "illusion" of future evenings at home alone with Fullerton: "I had my work, & you sat near the lamp, & read me a page of Chevrillon's article in the Revue de Paris—the article on Meredith that I had told you about. And as I followed you [in conversation]...ah, the illusion I had, of a life in which such evenings might be a dear, accepted habit!"(Price and McBride 671). Although this dream is a doomed one, the features which make it so attractive to Wharton (intimacy, conversation, light and warmth) animate the "romance" at the center of both the Love Diary and the novel.

THE INVALID SPOUSE

The novel is influenced by other aspects of Wharton's life in this period, for her husband's deteriorating health gave her a powerful reason to identify imaginatively with her most famous protagonist. (See biographical essay in the Introduction for details.) In the years between her writing of the 1907 French story and the 1911 English novel, she not only began and ended an extramarital affair but experienced the growing demands of a severely ill spouse. Shari Benstock describes the influence of this illness on the novel *Ethan Frome*: "Disillusioned with her lover, her husband in the throes of mental illness, Edith felt as tied to Teddy as Ethan Frome was to his bed-ridden wife, Zeena" (247). As early as the spring of 1908, Wharton was expressing concern about her husband's health and seeking help from various specialists. By the start of 1909, neither she nor Teddy's doctors could deny that he was suffering from mental illness rather than physical maladies such as gout or neurasthenia. Concerned about his precarious condition and the violent mood swings to which he was prone, she attempted to protect him by limiting their engagements in Paris and by curtailing all dinner parties and houseguests at their home in the Faubourg Saint-Germain. By the start of 1910, the year she began writing *Ethan Frome*, she was contending with the details of his breakdown in America and forced to acknowledge his complete dependence on her.

Wharton's letters from this period confirm the strain which she was experiencing as she tried to help a spouse who had become a patient. To Robert Grant, a friend of hers who had also known Teddy all of his life, she was willing to confide the frustration which she felt: "I can only watch passively, shelter Teddy as much as I can from worry, and from the curiosity and comments which are inevitable when a man in his condition attempts to live in the world, and be prepared for the fact that any day he may yield to some impulse like those which wrought such havoc in his life last summer" (Benstock 231). Unable to write with any consistency until late in the year, when Teddy was away for several months, she grew more and more tired through 1910 as she attempted to care for him and to accommodate the moods which he could no longer control. Coping at the same time with in-laws who denied the seriousness of Teddy's problems, she struggled to fulfill her duty to a husband making constant demands on her. In the following excerpt from a spring letter to Morton Fullerton, she vividly conveys the toll of her husband's illness:

The Whartons adroitly refuse to recognize the strain I am under, & the impossibility, for a person with nerves strung like mine, to go on leading indefinitely the life I am now leading. They say: "The responsibility rests with his wife—we merely reserve the right to criticize." *He* has only one thought—to be with me all day, every day. If I try to escape, he will follow; if I protest, & say I want to be left alone, they will say that I deserted him when he was ill.... — And if you knew, if you *knew*, what the days are, what the hours are, what our talks are, interminable repetitions of the same weary round of inanities & puerilities; & all with the knowledge definitely before me, put there by all the Drs, that what is killing me is doing him no good! (*Letters* 215)

Wharton's plaintive note about her own health and equilibrium was not misplaced, for several doctors registered their concern in this period over the effects of her husband's illness on her. When Teddy began anticipating his release from a Swiss sanitarium in July and planning his return to Paris, her doctor intervened and insisted that he instead travel for several months because she was weak and in need of "*grand repos physique et moral*" (Lewis 289). Laboring under the burden of her husband's illness, Wharton was exhausted as the decade drew to a close and freshly preoccupied with the constraints of her marriage.

In the midst of this personal crisis, Wharton returned imaginatively to the 1907 story of Hart and completed the novel *Ethan Frome*. When Teddy began an extended trip in November 1910 in the care of an employee whom she trusted, she seized the opportunity to resume her daily writing. The story which absorbed and invigorated her was that of Ethan Frome, a laconic figure whose predicament bore an uncanny resemblance to her own. Lewis suggests that the novel which resulted is an expression of Wharton's emotional life during several turbulent years:

But the great and durable vitality of the tale comes at last from the personal feelings Edith Wharton invested in it, the feelings by which she lived her narrative. *Ethan Frome* portrays her personal situation, as she had come to appraise it, carried to a far extreme, transplanted to a remote rural scene, and rendered utterly hopeless by circumstance. As she often did, Edith shifted the sexes in devising her three central characters. Like Edith Wharton, Ethan Frome is married to an ailing spouse a number of years older than he, and has been married for about the same length of time as Edith had been tied to Teddy. (309)

These parallels between the lives of the novelist and her protagonist supply a valuable context for the work's somber tone and climactic "smash up." Chafing against her own duty to an incurably ill spouse, Wharton could imagine no escape for her fictional counterpart in life. Ethan's late assessment of his situation is couched in terms which his creator knew too well: "He was a poor man, the husband of a sickly woman, whom his desertion would leave alone and destitute" (136). In her responsibility for a sick husband whom she did not love, Wharton identified closely with this New England farmer torn between his duty to an invalid and his desire for a soul mate.

"SALVATION IS THERE": THE PROCESS
OF COMPOSITION

Early in the summer of 1910, Wharton found herself freed temporarily of
Teddy and his unpredictable behavior. She returned to her daily regimen
with keen satisfaction, expressing to a friend the newfound importance
which she attached to her writing: "I am hard at work on a short novel
which I have taken up since Teddy went to Switzerland, & hope to have
time to get well started while I am here alone [in Paris]. It has been impossible to work except spasmodically these last months, & more & more I find
that Salvation is there & there only" (*Letters* 218). Eager as she was to give
herself to the discipline of her art after the turmoil of the past few years, she
was not able to work on the manuscript with any consistency before the start
of winter. When she resumed her writing in December, however, she concentrated on it happily for a six-week period. She wrote every morning and
read the day's work to Walter Berry every evening, later pointing out in her
autobiography that he too was acquainted with "the lives led in those half-
deserted villages before the coming of motor and telephone" (296). Lewis
notes that Wharton spent a "hardworking and relatively *un*social winter and
spring of 1911," reserving her best energies for her growing opus *Ethan
Frome* (*Letters* 229).

Wharton originally envisioned a shorter work than the completed novel
which she submitted to Scribner's, for she planned to write the story in a few
weeks' time. At the start of 1911, she wrote humorously to her confidant
Bernard Berenson about the unexpected length which *Ethan Frome* was
assuming:

I am driving harder and harder at that ridiculous nouvelle, which has grown into a
large long-legged hobbledehoy of a young novel. 20,000 long it is already, and
growing. I have to let its frocks down every day, and soon it will be in trousers!
However, I see an end, for I'm over the hard explanatory part, and the vitesse
acquise [acquired speed] is beginning to rush me along. The scene is laid at
Starkfield, Mass, and the nearest cosmopolis is called Shadd's Falls. It amuses
me to do that décor in the rue de Varenne. (*Letters* 232)

By the start of March, Wharton was describing the completed work to
Berenson as a "hybrid" of novel and short story (Lewis 296). She never
wavered in her expressions of delight with the work, and she singles it out in
her autobiography as "the book to the making of which I brought the
greatest joy and the fullest ease" (293). Unwilling to trust her own powers as
artist for much of her long career, Wharton nonetheless recognized the scale
of her achievement when she published *Ethan Frome*.

At the urging of Teddy's doctor, Wharton returned to the Mount for the
summer of 1911. Surrounded by her closest friends, she enjoyed her last
and best season there as installments of *Ethan Frome* appeared in *Scribner's*

Magazine. Buoyed by the enthusiastic responses of friends and critics to the work, her first novel in four years, she anticipated lively sales and healthy royalties. (She had already received $2,500 for serial rights and a $2,000 advance.) Yet sales proceeded sluggishly after the simultaneous publication of the novel in New York and London in September, and only forty-two hundred copies had been purchased by year's end. Frustrated by the pace of these sales, Wharton accused Scribner's of failing to advertise the novel appropriately and to maintain the quality which she demanded in printing. Although her editor was able to report sales of more than seven thousand copies by February 1912—and willing to issue an additional $1,000 advance payment—Wharton remained convinced that Scribner's had not served *Ethan Frome* well (Benstock 249). The result would be her eventual decision to leave Scribner's altogether for D. Appleton and Company, the publisher of her next novel, *The Reef*.

3

---·•◦•·---

CONTEXTS

Edith Wharton's long career straddled two centuries and several distinct literary movements. She came of age as the American romance was yielding to the realistic novel, and she continued writing through the decline of High Modernism. A disciplined reader who educated herself, she was thoroughly familiar with the converging streams of nineteenth-century American fiction and drew on uniquely American literary traditions as she wrote *Ethan Frome*. The result was a novel which is still widely regarded as the most American work of her career. In its attempt to evoke New England's symbolic landscape, *Ethan Frome* pays homage to the genius of Nathaniel Hawthorne. In its bleak portrayal of the shrinking New England village, the novel challenges the claims of contemporary realists associated with the local color school. And in its dramatization of the law of necessity governing the lives of its doomed characters, the novel explores the premises of late nineteenth-century naturalism. Wharton's accomplishment in the finished work is much more than a survey of developments in modern American fiction, of course. With the publication of *Ethan Frome* in 1911, Wharton assumed her own place as a major American writer in a rich tradition.[1]

NATHANIEL HAWTHORNE'S ROMANCES

Wrongly regarded as Henry James's protégée for much of her career, Wharton acknowledged a different influence as she began writing *Ethan Frome*. Weighing the life she observed in the isolated Berkshire villages surrounding her summer home, she turned imaginatively not to James but to Nathaniel Hawthorne. She appropriates a dominant image of Hawthorne's in the opening chapter of *Ethan Frome*, when her protagonist contemplates the "sky of iron" overhead (64). Lewis suggests the scale of this author's influence on the work: "Despite her early disclaimers, the spirit of Nathaniel Hawthorne pervades the New England landscape of the novella and lies behind the moral desolation of Ethan Frome—a desolation as complete in its special manner as that of his namesake, Hawthorne's Ethan Brand" (309). Author of the one undisputed masterpiece of nineteenth-century American fiction, Hawthorne was also New England's greatest chronicler. Renowned for his achievement in *The Scarlet Letter* (1850), he had already amassed an impressive body of short fiction in the collections *Twice-Told Tales* (1837) and *Mosses from an Old Manse* (1846) which preceded the novel. His short stories supply a densely textured history of the region which formed him, extending from the beginnings of the colonial period in "The Maypole of Merry Mount" to the verge of the Revolutionary War in "My Kinsman, Major Molineux." These poetic meditations on the legacy of the Puritan past are rooted in the same New England landscape dominating *Ethan Frome*.

Hawthorne's art provides a vibrant context for Wharton's novel on more than one level. The novel's awareness of Hawthorne, a figure inextricably tied to New England, immediately strengthens its claims on the region and its literature. Associated prominently with Old New York from the 1905 publication of *The House of Mirth*, Wharton always bristled at critics who were skeptical about her ability to portray life in New England.[2] She wrote of working conditions in the Lowell mills in the 1907 novel *The Fruit of the Tree*, and she devoted at least ten major stories ("The Angel at the Grave," "The Pretext") to late nineteenth-century life in New England. Two of the three manuscripts which she left unfinished at her death (*Mother Earth* and *New England*) were novels set in the same corner of western Massachusetts as *Ethan Frome*. Yet Wharton felt compelled to begin her introduction to the 1922 edition of *Ethan Frome* by reminding readers of the time she had spent in the region: "I had known something of New England village life long before I made my home in the same county as my imaginary Starkfield; though, during the years spent there, certain of its aspects became much more familiar to me" (Lauer and Wolff xi). Writing her autobiography in the 1930s, she continued to assert her thorough familiarity with the Berkshires of her fiction.

I wrote the tale [*Ethan Frome*] as it now stands, reading my morning's work aloud each evening to Walter Berry, who was as familiar as I was with the lives led in those half-deserted villages before the coming of motor and telephone. We talked the tale over page by page, so that its accuracy of "atmosphere" is doubly assured—and I mention this because not long since, in an article by an American literary critic, I saw "Ethan Frome" cited as an interesting example of a successful New England story written by someone who knew nothing of

New England! "Ethan Frome" was written after I had spent ten years in the hill-region where the scene is laid, during which years I had come to know well the aspect, dialect, and mental and moral attitude of the hill-people. (*Backward Glance* 296)

Here and elsewhere, Wharton staunchly defends the authenticity of her narrative's New England setting. Rejecting what she terms the "rose-and-lavender pages" of more sentimental contemporaries, she cites the austere fiction of Hawthorne as her precedent for *Ethan Frome (Backward Glance* 294).

Important as this literary continuity was for Wharton in 1910, she generally lacked sympathy for Hawthorne's vision. His romances are in the background of *Ethan Frome*, but their religious and political concerns are not Wharton's. Described by Q. D. Leavis as "critic and interpreter of American cultural history" (33), Hawthorne explores in all of his works the complex legacy of Calvinism and the illusion of progress at the heart of the American experience. Absorbed in the inner lives of characters shaped by explicitly American conditions, his fiction dramatizes the limits of fallen human nature. Convinced as she was that American Puritanism contributed nothing more than strained relations between men and women,[3] Wharton did not share Hawthorne's artistic preoccupation with human frailty and sinfulness. Reading her friend William Crary Brownell's 1908 essay on the scale of Hawthorne's achievement, she could muster only tart words:

My only two quarrels with you are for calling the Scarlet L. "our one prose masterpiece"—I'd so much rather we had more than that one; and for saying that his prose has a classic quality. It seems to me about as classic as a bare hotel parlour furnished only with bentwood chairs.

But, oh, the good things you say by the way! How the *marble* was what he saw in sculpture (that is the key to so much of him); how he dwelt apart, and was therefore taken for a star; how there can hardly be a more barren state than revery for the production for anything beyond "conceits." (Lewis 237)

Lewis suggests that this criticism reflects the ambition of a young author attempting to advance her career—and claim her own place in the tradition—by denigrating the work of another (237). Uncomfortably aware of Hawthorne's long shadow as she refined her craft, Wharton nonetheless chose to identify herself with him as she wrote *Ethan Frome*. For Candace Waid, Wharton's temporary allegiance to Hawthorne at this juncture is "little more than a gesture meant to establish the primacy in American literature of the dark and stylized view she promoted of New England" (7).

The most obvious allusions to Hawthorne in Wharton's work are the names of two of the novel's three main characters. Writing her first draft of this story as a 1907 French exercise, Wharton sketched a triangle consisting of a young farmer named Hart, his wife Anna and her cousin Mattie.

Returning imaginatively to this situation in 1910, she renamed the married couple after two of Hawthorne's more memorable characters. Judith Fryer emphasizes the deep loneliness of these particular characters of Hawthorne's, and contends that this trait preoccupied Wharton as she planned her story of New England (180). The figures Wharton chose from Hawthorne's romances both take their own lives, thus completing the act which Ethan Frome and Mattie Silver unsuccessfully attempt at the climax of *Ethan Frome.*

Wharton's Hart became the namesake of the restless wanderer Ethan Brand, described by Cynthia Griffin Wolff as "the only other notable Ethan in American literature" (159). The eponymous protagonist of the 1851 story "Ethan Brand: A Chapter from an Abortive Romance" begins life in a small Berkshire village similar to Frome's Starkfield but then spends nearly twenty years traveling in search of the Unpardonable Sin. As the story opens, Brand is returning to Mount Graylock and the remote lime kiln which he once tended every night. Quizzed by his coarse successor about his adventures, he wearily confirms that he has found the Unpardonable Sin which he sought: " 'It is a sin that grew within my own breast.... A sin that grew nowhere else! The sin of an intellect that triumphed over God, and sacrificed everything to its own mighty claims! The only sin that deserves a recompense of immortal agony!' " (1057). Exemplar of the dangerous split between head and heart which recurs in Hawthorne's fiction, Brand is characterized by the completeness of his isolation. The sensitive young boy who views him last is moved to tears by his "intuition of the bleak and terrible loneliness in which this man had enveloped himself" (1063). At the story's climax, Brand contemplates the burning lime fire and recalls how he forfeited his place in the human community by pursuing his abstract quest single-mindedly. His final act is to plunge into the hot fires of the kiln, leaving behind a heart of marble.

Wharton was thinking of another defiant character of Hawthorne's when she discarded the name Anna in favor of Zeena. Homely diminutive notwithstanding, Zeena Frome is named for the exotic center of Hawthorne's 1852 novel *The Blithedale Romance.* Although each Zenobia finds herself part of an uncomfortable triangle—with a noticeably younger woman—Hawthorne's and Wharton's novels offer few other parallels. His Zenobia is a stunning woman who helps to shape the utopian experiment underway at Silas Foster's farm. (The inspiration for this figure is widely believed to be Margaret Fuller, enthusiastic supporter of the Transcendental experiment at Brook Farm which attracted Hawthorne for a time.) Zenobia is a founding member of Blithedale, a philanthropist and an accomplished writer who has taken the name of the famous Queen of Palmyra who resisted the Roman Empire in the third century. The novel steadily characterizes her as a gifted figure of regal stature: "She was, indeed, an admirable figure of a woman, just on the hither verge of her richest maturity, with a combination of features which it is safe to call remarkably beautiful" (645). An eloquent advocate of women's equality with men, Zenobia devotes great energy to the utopian project underway and looks confidently to a future with the community's leader, Hollingsworth. When he rejects her unexpectedly in favor of her shy younger sister, Zenobia is formidable in her grief and her contempt for his egotism. Desperately unhappy, she takes her leave of Blithedale Farm and drowns herself in the river.

Through the fates of his characters Ethan and Zenobia, Hawthorne develops a major theme of his fiction. Their experiences within the different works reveal the destructive consequences of isolation for the human person. Hawthorne's familiar metaphor of the "magnetic chain of humanity" expresses the alternative, a life bound up in others within a larger community. Near the end of "Ethan Brand," the protagonist's reflection on the condition of his heart is organized by this image: "That indeed had withered—had contracted—had hardened—had perished! It had ceased to partake of the universal throb. He had lost his hold of the magnetic chain of humanity. He was no longer a brother man, opening the chambers or the dungeons of our common nature by the key of holy sympathy"(1064). Hawthorne's fiction is filled with characters that exist apart and suffer similar losses. The title character of "Wakefield" becomes "the Outcast of the Universe" when he indulges his egotism and chooses to disappear from his own life (298); the goodly Reverend Hooper of "The Minister's Black Veil" places himself where "love or sympathy could never reach him" when he dons the piece of black crape for the benefit of his parishioners (380). Hester Prynne, Hawthorne's most famous character, spends seven long years alone in a "moral wilderness; as vast, as intricate and shadowy, as the untamed forest" (290). The isolation which she and Arthur Dimmesdale each experience within the Puritan society of *The Scarlet Letter* is treated as the dark consequence of their sin against the community.

The toll of isolation is a prominent theme of *Ethan Frome* as well, though Wharton frames the problem differently. Focusing on the inner life of her protagonist with an intensity which recalls Hawthorne, she explores the psychological dimensions of Frome's situation. Wolff comments on this distinction in the following way: "Wharton was not interested in sin, but she was interested in the effect of isolation upon the workings of man's emotional life: thus Ethan Frome is related to Ethan Brand; but his deadening isolation is in the cold world of unloved and unloving inner emptiness—a world of depression, loneliness, and slow starvation" (159–60). Trapped for most of his adult life in silence and loneliness, Frome enters the novel as "but the ruin of a man" (63). Through his physical deformity—and the red gash branded across his forehead[4]—Wharton expresses a full measure of the suffering which he has endured in frozen Starkfield.

His farm is another symbolic projection of his solitude, his depleted farmhouse "the image of his own shrunken body":

Abreast of the schoolhouse the road forked, and we dipped down a lane to the left, between hemlock boughs bent inward to their trunks by the weight of the snow. I had often walked that way on Sundays, and knew that the solitary roof showing through bare branches near the bottom of the hill was that of Frome's saw-mill. It looked examinate enough, with its idle wheel looming above the black stream dashed with yellow-white spume, and its cluster of sheds sagging under their white load. (71)

Taking in the desolation of this setting, the narrator grows in understanding of Frome and the life he has led since the sledding accident (63). The long flashback which follows is framed by the visiting engineer's acknowledgment that Frome moves in a "depth of moral isolation too remote for casual access" (69). No longer connected to others by the magnetic chain of humanity, Wharton's protagonist cannot escape the desperate loneliness of Hawthorne's earlier New Englanders.

LOCAL COLOR REALISM

No other work of Wharton's career sparked the lively debate which attended the publication of *Ethan Frome*, and the author continued to defend her intentions in the novel more than twenty years later. A New Yorker connected to Boston by marriage, Wharton was ever confident that her ten summers in residence at the Mount ensured the credibility of her stories and novels set in New England. Her repeated answer to objections about the accuracy of her work was to distinguish between the life which she observed firsthand in the Berkshires and the life recorded in works of local color realism. The gap between the two was wide, according to Wharton, and one consequence was distrust of her own New England fiction. In her introduction to the 1922 edition of *Ethan Frome*, she makes clear that she doubted contemporary portraits of New England long before she settled for a time in the Berkshires:

Even before that final initiation [to New England village life], however, I had had an uneasy sense that the New England of fiction bore little—except a vague botanical and dialectical—resemblance to the harsh and beautiful land as I had seen it. Even the abundant enumeration of sweet-fern, asters and mountain-laurel, and the conscientious reproduction of the vernacular, left me with the feeling that the outcropping granite had in both cases been overlooked. I give the impression merely as a personal one; it accounts for "Ethan Frome," and may, to some readers, in a measure justify it. (Lauer and Wolff 3)

Wharton presents the neglected crags of New England as her justification for the method of *Ethan Frome*. She extends this metaphor later in the introduction, treating her effort to root out sentimentality and falsehood as essential to the successful creation of her characters, "granite outcroppings; but half-emerged from the soil, and scarcely more articulate" (Lauer and Wolff 3).

Discussing *Ethan Frome* in her autobiography, Wharton assigns this same primitive quality to much of the region. She supports the characterization by recounting her inspiration for *Summer*, the 1917 novel so closely connected to *Ethan Frome* in her thinking that she once called it "Hot Ethan" (*Letters* 385). Set in a Berkshire village no larger or more vital than Starkfield, *Summer* features a dissolute group of outlaws and outcasts living at a remove on "the Mountain" (actually Bear Mountain, twelve miles from the Mount). A late scene in the novel depicting the drunken funeral of the protagonist Charity Royall's mother emphasizes the squalid circumstances of this mountain colony. Intended to shock the reader, the sequence is inspired by the experience of a Lenox rector called to assist at the burial of "a woman of evil reputation" in the mountains (*Backward Glance* 296). Wharton presents this lurid tableau as all too revealing of the New England she sought to capture in *Ethan Frome* as well as *Summer*:

For years I had wanted to draw life as it really was in the derelict mountain villages of New England, a life even in my time, and a thousandfold more a generation earlier, utterly unlike that seen through the rose-coloured spectacles of my predecessors, Mary Wilkins and Sarah Orne Jewett. In those days the snow-bound villages of Western Massachusetts were still grim places, morally and physically: insanity, incest and slow mental and moral starvation were hidden away behind the paintless wooden house-fronts of the long village street, or in the isolated farm-houses on the neighbouring hills; and Emily Bronte would have found as savage tragedies in our remoter villages as on her Yorkshire moors. (*Backward Glance* 294–95)

The invocation of *Wuthering Heights* underscores Wharton's ambition for her own New England stories and novels. Openly derisive of the fiction of regional writers, Wharton insists that her bleak portrayal of village life in *Ethan Frome* is the superior work of literary realism. Exploring Wharton's views of regional writers in her study *Resisting Regionalism*, Donna M. Campbell argues that *Ethan Frome* and *Summer* constitute the author's most determined effort to revise New England's local color fiction (151).

Wharton's resistance notwithstanding, the region's stories and novels were an important part of a larger literary project underway following the Civil War. Associated most closely with the three writers William Dean Howells, Mark Twain and Henry James, the American realistic novel which emerged in the 1870s and 1880s rejected the idealism and the elevated language of earlier romances. Seeking to capture the often dissonant rhythms of a rapidly changing postwar society, representative works of realism such as *Adventures of Huckleberry Finn* (1881), *The Portrait of a Lady* (1881) and *The Rise of Silas Lapham* (1885) gave new emphasis to recognizable characters, contemporary mores and appropriate speech. Near the center of the novel *The Rise of Silas Lapham*, a sympathetic character deplores the excesses of sentimental fiction and argues that novelists need to strive for verisimilitude in characterization as well as plot: " 'Commonplace? The commonplace is just that light, impalpable, airy essence which they've never gotten into their confounded books yet. The novelist who could interpret the common feelings of commonplace people would have the answer to 'the riddle of the painful earth' on his tongue' " (187–88). In his 1891 essay "Criticism and Fiction," Howells underscores the realistic novel's deepening interest in psychology by asserting that "fidelity to experience and probability of motive are essential conditions of a great imaginative literature" (*Criticism* 15). Eschewing the extravagant symbolism of *The Scarlet Letter* and the epic struggles of *Moby-Dick*, the realistic novel which he championed embraces the world of the quotidian and reveals the concerns of a rising middle class.

Late nineteenth-century fiction from specific regions of the country helped to ease this transition between romance and realism. Commonly identified with the growing city, modern American realism also influenced works set in coastal Maine villages and California mining camps. Eric Sundquist argues that these regional stories and novels were a vital component of the literary movement reshaping American fiction:

A simple division between the urban realism that accompanied the growth of industrial America in the post-Civil War period and the several regional literatures that flourished at the same time would lose sight of the complex aesthetic, social, and economic entanglements between them. If we instead judge realism from the 1870s through the early 1900s as a developing series of responses to the transformation of land into capital, of raw materials into products, of agrarian values into urban values, and of private experience into public property, then the city appears as one region among others, part of the national network of modernization actualized as much by the ties of language and literature as by new railroad lines and telegraph wires. (501)

Rapid expansion of communication and transportation in the postwar years both connected formerly isolated regions and exposed differences among them. Like their urban counterparts in the East, regional writers in different pockets of the country discarded exaggeration and sentimentality as they attempted a vernacular literature which expressed their particular customs and concerns.

Hamlin Garland, Midwestern author of the collection *Main-Travelled Roads* (1891), offers a memorable description of this literature in his work *Crumbling Idols*: "Local color in a novel means that it has such quality of texture and background that it could not have been written in any other place or by any one else than a native" (53–54). The rich sense of place which

Garland attributes to local color realism infused a growing body of stories throughout the 1880s and the early 1890s, with picturesque landscapes from across the nation assuming new prominence. The rise in popularity of the local color story is traditionally tied to Bret Harte, whose story "The Luck of Roaring Camp" was first printed in *Overland Monthly* in 1868 (and then promptly reprinted in a host of other newspapers). Harte's colorful account of a California mining camp was soon followed by other, better works from the South, the West and the East. The form of the short story proved more congenial to the aims of local color than that of the novel or the poem, in part because of the episodic nature of works concentrated on what Claude Simpson calls "provincial manners": "This is not to say that the local colorist lacks interest in the more universal aspects of human nature, but rather that his major emphasis is on *differentiae*, not on the generic" (2–3). Throughout the 1870s and 1880s, magazines such as *Atlantic*, *Harper's* and *Scribner's* were filled with regional stories, and the most successful of these works were collected in more than one hundred fifty volumes by the turn of the century (Simpson 8). Although the appeal of local color fiction waned in the 1890s, its best practitioners satisfied the conditions of literary realism by rendering the speech, the gestures and the values of unexceptional Americans living in distinctive places.

A strong motive for writing local color fiction was the authors' desire to preserve a way of life threatened by an increasingly modern, technological society. Carlos Baker explains, "At a crucial point in American history, when old faces, manners, customs, recipes, styles, attitudes, and prejudices were undergoing rapid change or total extirpation, they seized and perpetuated, through the medium of fictional character, the cultural landscape: the native idiom, the still unravished rural peace, the feel and flavor of things as they were, and would never be again" (861). The New England writer Sarah Orne Jewett (1849–1909) prized her relation to an earlier period in Maine's history, when her own South Berwick boasted thriving trades of shipbuilding and whaling. Generally acknowledged as the most accomplished writer of the local color movement, Jewett acquired her understanding of the region and its people by accompanying her cultivated father, the town doctor, on his rounds. When she began writing, he offered her advice which guided her throughout her successful career: "Don't try to write *about* people and things, tell them just as they are!" Jewett published her first story at twenty in the *Atlantic Monthly*, and, at Howells' urging, collected the sketches which followed in the volume *Deephaven* (1877). Like many of Jewett's later stories, *Deephaven* captures the goodness of a lost time as it conveys the strength of men and women still living on the Maine coast.

Jewett published her greatest work twenty years later, as the local color movement drew to a close. Her novel *The Country of the Pointed Firs* (1896) is widely regarded as the finest achievement of nineteenth-century regional fiction,[5] meditating as it does on the distinctive features of both the coastline and the community. A series of related sketches rather than a traditional novel, *The Country of the Pointed Firs* is unified by the author's vision of everyday life in Maine (Matthiessen 101). Its setting is the fictional Dunnet Landing, a formerly thriving town which has lost its maritime economy. The narrator, a city-bred outsider who visits for a summer, learns the full measure of this loss from Captain Littlepage:

In the old days, a good part o' the best men here knew a hundred ports and something of the way folks lived in them. They saw the world for themselves, and like's not their wives and children saw it with them. They may not have had the best of knowledge to carry with 'em sight-seein', but they were acquainted with foreign lands an' their laws, an' could see sense o' proportion. Yes, they lived more dignified, and their houses were better within an' without. Shipping's a terrible loss to this part o' New England from a social point o' view, ma'am. (20)

Through these words of the long-retired captain, Jewett identifies a major theme of the book. The "terrible loss" which New England has suffered since the Civil War is clear in the shrunken dimensions of Dunnet Landing—and in the isolation of so many men and women connected to it. The lonely widower Elijah Tilley and the recluse Joanna of Shell-heap Island are two of the novel's more vibrant studies of figures who live apart in "continual loneliness" (122).

The novel pays sympathetic attention to these figures in retreat, but it also celebrates the strength of several remarkable women close to the center of Dunnet Landing. The narrator lodges for the summer with Almira Todd, a widowed herbalist who assists the local doctor in healing the community. Mrs. Todd reminds her boarder of an ancient prophetess or seer, but this kind-hearted character also embodies Yankee traits of self-sufficiency, independence and practicality (Westbrook 62). Mrs. Todd's characterization is extended and deepened by the narrator's presentation of her mother, Mrs. Blackett. Accompanying Mrs. Todd on a visit to tiny Green Island where Mrs. Blackett lives with her son William, the narrator marvels at the intact community which she finds there. These same qualities of hospitality and warmth shape the climax of *The Country of the Pointed Firs*, when the narrator accompanies Mrs. Todd and Mrs. Blackett to the annual reunion of the Bowden family. Imbuing this festive day with "transfiguring powers" (96), Jewett honors the characters that assemble and affirms the bonds they maintain despite the distances which separate them throughout the year.

The regional fiction of Mary Wilkins Freeman (1852–1930) casts a darker light on the lives of late nineteenth-century New Englanders. Although Wharton failed to distinguish between Jewett and Freeman in her criticism of their work, important differences separate these popular local colorists. The personal circumstances of the two women contrasted sharply, for

Freeman was raised in western Massachusetts in poverty so acute that her mother was eventually forced to become a servant in a minister's household. The Wilkins family moved to Brattleboro, Vermont in 1867, as postwar conditions in rural Randolph, Massachusetts steadily deteriorated following the collapse of its shoemaking industry. After completing her formal education with a year of study at Mount Holyoke and publishing her first story in *Harper's*, Mary Wilkins returned to the village of Randolph and remained there until her marriage in 1902 to Dr. Charles Freeman of Metchuen, New Jersey. Praising her ability to convey "the desolation of the Yankee ebb-tide," Van Wyck Brooks suggests that Randolph was a formative influence on her realism: "Randolph at that time was not a suburb. It was a fading Yankee village, and this was the moribund village,—the symbol of hundreds of others,—that appeared in her stories. In its dilapidated houses dwelt a race that seemed to be dying, as shell-fish on a shoal that is seldom reached by the tide wither and perish at last when deprived of water" (465–66). A prolific writer whose career spanned nearly fifty years, Freeman set her most representative stories in declining New England villages and towns cut off from the prosperity and the energy of the rising American city.

Freeman published fourteen collections of stories in her lifetime, with her finest work contained in the early volumes *A Humble Romance and Other Stories* (1887) and *A New England Nun and Other Stories* (1891). The stories in these two collections established her reputation and defined her center of interest as a regional writer. Adept at evoking the "fading Yankee village," Freeman took even greater care with the struggles of its isolated inhabitants. Her plots are deliberately slight, allowing her to fix the reader's attention on the inner lives of her protagonists (Reichardt 21). These protagonists are most often lonely or forgotten women whose experiences are filtered through the ironic detachment of her narrators. Simpson comments on Freeman's impressive control over her material: "The stark effect of her stories is enhanced by an objectivity which allows the action to unfold without the machinery of the 'frame' or the presiding personality of the author planted between story and reader. The minor tragedies reflect poverty of opportunity, or of intellect, or of energy, and Mrs. Freeman rarely throws a sentimental veil of pathos over the scene" (64). The elderly Shattuck sisters of "A Mistaken Charity" (1887) illustrate Freeman's talent for presenting her characters' plight without enlarging or romanticizing their natures. Despite their need, Charlotte and Harriet spurn the comforts of the "Old Ladies' Home" to which an officious neighbor sends them. Preferring their liberty—and the flavor of pumpkins and currants from their own meager garden—they flee the city poorhouse for the dilapidated cottage where they belong.

Freeman's best stories depict the efforts of women to preserve their independence in a variety of circumstances. "The Revolt of 'Mother'" (1890) treats this struggle wryly, relating Sarah Penn's campaign when her husband of forty years builds yet another spacious barn finer than the house in which she has raised their two children. Claiming the new building as the family's home in his absence, she calmly dictates her terms upon his return: " 'The house wa'n't fit for us to live in any longer, an' I made up my mind I wa'n't goin' to stay there. I've done my duty by you forty year, an' I'm goin' to do it now; but I'm goin' to live here. You've got to put in some windows and partitions, an' you'll have to buy some furniture' " (77). A stunned Adoniram Penn can only assent meekly to his wife's wishes, for he has been forced to take new measure of her. Freeman's younger protagonists often face more formidable obstacles, particularly if they choose to remain unmarried. Louisa Ellis of "A New England Nun" (1887) has waited fourteen years for her fiancé Joe Dagget to make his fortune in Australia, only to discover when he returns to marry her that she prefers the "happy, solitary life" (27) which she has led since her mother and brother died. The impoverished title character of "Louisa" (1890) struggles through a summer to feed her mother and grandfather from her rocky garden, but rebuffs the wealthy Jonathan Nye each time that he attempts to court her. She experiences quiet joy at story's end nonetheless, when she learns that the position of village schoolteacher is once again hers. Her triumph over circumstance is modest—like most Freeman victories—but undeniably her own.

Freeman's interest in the pressure of circumstance on her protagonists illuminates unexpected affinities between Wharton's art and her own. Less inclined than Freeman to honor the capacity for stoical endurance in New Englanders, Wharton nonetheless evinces her concern with the physical and psychological privation of their characters' lives. And in her view of the region as a desiccated place, Wharton resembles Freeman much more closely than Jewett. Nancy R. Leach criticizes the absence of authentic dialect and detail in Wharton's New England stories and novels but acknowledges the author's grasp of the prevailing situation in pockets of the region, "such as that in the mountain villages like Starkfield, North Dormer, and Highridge, with their lack of culture and economic opportunity, rapidly being depopulated by the more ambitious and talented young people, and serving instead as a refuge for the old people and those defeated in spirit" (96). Wharton's short stories about late nineteenth-century New England extend beyond these rural villages to include the provincial college towns of "The Recovery" (1901) and "The Pretext" (1908). Her characterizations are consistent in both milieus, however, for she imagines in each setting figures who cannot escape the past, such as Paulina of "The Angel at the Grave" (1901) who turns her family home into a museum and devotes her lonely days to tending the memory of her philosopher-grandfather.

The unlikely figure of Harmon Gow in *Ethan Frome* conveys Wharton's view of such an existence when he says, " 'Most of the smart ones get away' " (64). His words shape our introduction to Wharton's most famous protagonist, of course, but they also reflect her sustained criticism of nineteenth-century New England as a beautiful but lifeless place. Carol J. Singley argues that the author's shifting regard for the region influenced *Ethan Frome* directly. "Wharton had a complicated relationship with New England. She both reveled in its natural splendor and decried its austerity; this ambivalence helps to explain how she could produce a novel of such technical beauty and thematic gloom" (110). This complicated attitude toward the region which she visited for so many years inevitably colored her views of its more prominent artists, her predecessor Hawthorne and her contemporaries Jewett and Freeman. Convinced of the dangerous legacy of Puritanism, Wharton saw only the severity of life within Hawthorne's Massachusetts Bay Colony. Perceiving the sharp limits of Berkshire village life, Wharton reacted against the picturesque aspects of Jewett's and Freeman's local color fiction. She regarded her most successful New England novel as a corrective, contrasting Calvinist duty with passion and replacing scenic landscapes with a destitute farmhouse and a looming elm tree.

4

IDEAS

Although *Ethan Frome* remains Wharton's most famous novel, it is often treated as an anomaly among her major works of fiction. It is set in a remote village in rural Massachusetts, a sharp contrast to the fashionable Old New York society at the center of so many of her novels. It recounts the experience of a taciturn farmer cut off from regular contact with his neighbors, in a spare volume unlike any of Wharton's multilayered novels of manners. Yet these differences of subject and form should not obscure the ways in which *Ethan Frome* pursues familiar concerns of the author's. The reduced circumstances of the title character are never intended to define his predicament but to convey Wharton's view of modern New England. The larger problem which the novel confronts is not poverty but moral isolation, an inescapable reality for one Wharton protagonist after another. In her depiction of the desperate loneliness of the three figures trapped in the Frome farmhouse, Wharton develops several of the themes which preoccupied her imaginatively throughout her career.

A SKY OF IRON: NINETEENTH-CENTURY DETERMINISM

In Chapter I, a young and vigorous Ethan Frome strides through a cold winter's night to collect Mattie Silver from a church dance and return her safely home. This first chapter begins not with Ethan or Mattie, however, but with their surroundings. Wharton takes care to establish the natural limits of their world in the novel's opening, from the two feet of snow dwarfing the village of Starkfield to the "sky of iron" overhead (75). Glittering stars form Orion and the Dipper in this "metallic dome" (75), an unyielding expanse also described as the "iron heavens" (87). Impressed by the stillness and clarity of the night itself, Ethan uses a term which he learned in college to describe his sensations. "'It's like being in an exhausted receiver,' he thought" (75). Seeking a way to express what he feels, Ethan imagines that he is trapped within the bell jar of a physics experiment. The narrator attributes this simile of Ethan's to the lingering effect of his scientific studies, noting that "though they had not gone far enough to be of much practical use they had fed his fancy and made him aware of huge cloudy meanings behind the daily face of things" (75–76). Yet the meaning which Ethan assigns to the quality of the night air reflects much more than the play of his imagination. His early thoughts of being part of a scientific experiment anticipate a major theme of the novel, for Ethan is characterized increasingly as a figure trapped in a world of immutable natural laws.

Associated prominently with the literary realism which began to reshape American fiction in the decades following the Civil War, Wharton was also receptive to the premises of naturalistic fiction. A writer attentive throughout her career to the pressure of circumstance on character, she adapted certain essential features of naturalism as she wrote *Ethan Frome*. As an avid reader of continental fiction she was familiar with the two different strands of nineteenth-century literary naturalism, European and American. The single European most important to this literary movement was the French writer Emile Zola (1840–1902), whose interest in modern advances in medicine and science inspired his influential treatise, *The Experimental Novel* (1880). A journalist as well as a novelist, Zola argued that fiction should be governed by modern scientific principles in its depictions of society. Richard Lehan explains, "Zola wanted the novelist to function like a scientist—to observe nature and social data, to reject supernatural explanations of the physical world, to reject absolute standards of morality and free will, and to reveal nature and human experience as a deterministic and mechanistic process—by which he meant controlled by scientific explanations of matter" (177). Through novels such as *L'Assommoir* (1877), *Nana* (1880) and *Germinal* (1885), Zola examined the lower tiers of French society during the Second Empire and sought to demonstrate the conditioning effects of heredity and environment on the individual.

Zola's method attracted widespread interest among American novelists of the 1890s. Writers such as Frank Norris, Theodore Dreiser and Jack London found in naturalism a liberating alternative to the realism of William Dean Howells. Journalists like Zola, they set out to capture the underside of the American experience at century's end—and to demonstrate that individuals were less responsible for their behavior than earlier novels claimed. In his 1896 essay "Zola as a Romantic Writer," Norris makes these aims explicit: "Terrible things must happen to the characters of the naturalistic tale. They must be twisted from the ordinary, wrenched out from the quiet, uneventful round of every-day life, and flung into the throes of a vast and terrible drama that works itself out in unleashed passions, in blood, and in sudden death" (72). For Norris and a number of his contemporaries, Zola's determinism signified an important advance over realism, one with sweeping implications for character and theme as well as plot.[1] Intent on portraying the harsh conditions their characters faced, they rejected the prevailing view of the human person in classic literary realism and replaced moral responsibility with weakness or compulsion. The individual in the naturalistic novel is thus a "wisp in the wind,"[2] subject to natural laws and forces which he can neither understand nor control.

The transformation of the United States from rural republic to industrial world power during the Gilded Age was another strong influence on emerging American naturalism. Lee Clark Mitchell suggests that naturalism's emphasis on the conditions or traits determining human behavior supplied many American writers with a new way of understanding the welter of late nineteenth-century life (526). Novelists beginning their careers in the last decade of the century contemplated a society profoundly different from the one which formed them, for the technological advances of the postwar years wrought vast changes in countryside and city alike. Naturalism served their efforts to protest the scale of these changes and to dramatize the consequences for increasingly anonymous individuals. Donald Pizer points out the wider implication which these writers perceived in the nation's modern identity: "The realization by the generation coming of age in the 1890s that American life had changed radically since the Civil War helped compromise a key aspect of the American Dream—the faith that America guaranteed all men the free and just pursuit of self-fulfillment and of the good life" (17). Naturalistic works such as Stephen Crane's *Maggie: A Girl of the Streets* (1893) and Theodore Dreiser's *Sister Carrie* (1900) expose the squalid living conditions of the overcrowded and inhospitable cities created by the American industrial revolution.[3] Upton Sinclair's novel *The Jungle* (1906) shocks readers with its account of horrendous practices in a Chicago slaughter house, as well as its depiction of the brutal treatment meted out to immigrants seeking a better life in America. These representative works of naturalism are shaped by the conviction that the unlimited possibility at the center of the American experience has been depleted, with the individual left to struggle ineffectually in the industrial era.

Social Darwinism made the philosophy of determinism even more compelling for a number of writers, confirming as it did the limitations placed on the individual within a world of matter. The United States responded more enthusiastically to *The Origin of the Species* (1859) than Charles Darwin's own England,[4] and efforts to apply evolutionary theory to society abounded for the last three decades of the nineteenth century. The philosopher Herbert Spencer became an even more influential figure than Darwin in American circles, and successive volumes of his *Synthetic Philosophy* (1860—) appeared to offer the reading public a cohesive scientific alternative to the cosmology of Christian revelation. As Richard Hofstadter observes, Spencer's theories shaped American discourse throughout the Gilded Age:

In the three decades after the Civil War it was impossible to be active in any field of intellectual work without mastering Spencer. Almost every American philosopher thinker of first or second rank—notably James, Royce, Dewey, Bowne, Harris, Howison, and McCosh—had to reckon with Spencer at some time. He had a vital influence upon most of the founders of American sociology, especially Ward, Cooley, Giddings, Small, and Sumner. "I imagine that nearly all of us who took up sociology between 1870, say, and 1890 did so at the instigation of Spencer," acknowledged Cooley. (*Social Darwinism* 33)

Spencer's effect on the period's fiction was less direct but undeniable, for his applications of Darwinian science to society seemed to explain the rampant competition of postwar America. The famous phrase which he coined, "survival of the fittest," gave American naturalists their metaphor for the plight of the alienated individual within an indifferent order (Pizer 18). The widely circulating language and assumptions of social Darwinism came to distinguish American naturalism of the 1890s from European naturalism of the 1870s, and major writers (Dreiser, London, Garland among them) made explicit in their novels and memoirs their debt to Spencer.

    Wharton herself was fascinated by what she called "the wonder-world of nineteenth century science," describing in her autobiography the excitement she felt when her friend Egerton Winthrop introduced her to the works of Darwin, Spencer, Huxley and a host of evolutionary theorists (*Backward Glance* 94). She went on to pay homage to Darwin by naming her 1904 story collection, *The Descent of Man*, for his 1871 work of the same name on natural selection. A serious intellectual, she followed closely developments in modern science and (inevitably) wrote fiction which revealed the influence of both Darwin and Spencer on her thought. Wharton's familiar setting of Old New York, for example, often serves as arena for the Darwinian struggle between a desiccated upper class and a brash, rising middle class. A number of critics have commented on this Darwinian dimension of Wharton's novels, particularly as it shapes the role of environment in each work.[5] Her biographer Lewis emphasizes that her growing interest in naturalism's view of "the implacable power of the environment" was bound up in her understanding of evolution: "Those fictional figures of hers who struggle pathetically against their stifling surroundings are belated offsprings of the tutelage of Egerton Winthrop—a combination, as it were, of Flaubert's *Madame Bovary* and the teachings of Herbert Spencer" (56–57). Dramatizing the way such surroundings confine and limit the individual, Wharton reflects the pervasiveness of determinism of the 1890s.

    Written during a period when Wharton herself felt hopelessly trapped, *Ethan Frome* is a potent examination of the naturalist outlook. From the opening pages of the prologue, the novel characterizes its protagonist as someone who has been denied a full life. The narrator is arrested by his first sight of Ethan, a ruined figure distinguished by "the careless powerful look he had, in spite of a lameness checking each step like the jerk of a chain" (63). Harmon Gow, the first choric figure to speak of Ethan's circumstances, supplies details which confirm the aptness of this simile. Many others have fled the isolated village of Starkfield, but Ethan remains a captive there twenty-four years after the mysterious "smash up" (63). Questioned about Ethan's dispirited manner, Gow replies in words which haunt the narrator and deepen his curiosity: " 'Guess he's been in Starkfield too many winters. Most of the smart ones get away' " (64). The driver brings this brief conversation to a close by volunteering the circumstances which have trapped Ethan in the village for so many years. Long before the accident which crippled him—and tethered him more firmly in place—Ethan remained behind to care first for his sick parents, and then for his ailing wife. An only son, he had no alternative but to abandon his studies in Worcester when his father fell ill and to tend the family farm in Starkfield.

The novel brings out clearly the severe limitations of the village in which Ethan is trapped, a place whose very name evokes a bleak open space. Contemplating the tyranny of winter in such a remote setting, the narrator uses charged language to describe what he perceives as "the deadness of the community" under snow and ice (65). As he considers the superior transportation and communication now connecting the small towns and villages of the Berkshires, he imagines how much quieter and emptier winter months were for Ethan twenty-four years earlier: "I began to see what life there—or rather its negation—must have been in Ethan Frome's young manhood" (65). Experiencing the "sluggish pulse" of the village during his stay, the narrator develops an extended metaphor comparing Starkfield in winter to a garrison under siege. "Twenty years earlier the means of resistance must have been far fewer, and the enemy in command of almost all the lines of access between the beleaguered villages; and, considering these things, I felt the sinister force of Harmon's phrase: 'Most of the smart ones get away.' But if that were the case, how could any combination of obstacles have hindered the flight of a man like Ethan Frome?" (66). Musing on the lifelessness of icebound Starkfield, the narrator simply cannot imagine the conditions which would trap a superior figure there year after year.

In her narrator's search for that "combination of obstacles" which has held Ethan captive in a remote village, Wharton is exploring the premises of naturalism. Her protagonist is defined by his potential for a richer, more purposeful life, by what Blake Nevius calls "the suggestion of his useful, even heroic possibilities" (119). Ethan once aspired to a life like the narrator's, for he studied science in Worcester and seized the opportunity to work for a time as an engineer in Florida. Recalled to Starkfield after his father's accident, he continued to nurse his ambitions for a different life in a larger, busier sphere and to manifest his deep appreciation for beauty. Working long hours to sustain the family farm and mill, he retreated in the evenings to the small room behind the parlor dedicated to more intellectual pursuits: "Here he had nailed up shelves for his books, built himself a box-sofa out of boards and a mattress, laid out his papers on a kitchen-table, hung on the rough plaster wall an engraving of Abraham Lincoln and a calendar with 'Thoughts from the Poets,' and tried, with these meager properties, to produce some likeness to the study of a 'minister' who had been kind to him and lent him books when he was at Worcester" (129). In this sanctuary all his own, Ethan tried to maintain some connection to the life he enjoyed in college and dreamed of a world beyond the barn and the fields. He preserved these ambitions through his mother's slow decline, eventually marrying Zeena with the firm intention of escaping Starkfield and beginning again elsewhere. "He had always wanted to be an engineer and to live in towns, where there were lectures and big libraries and 'fellows doing things'" (98). These inchoate plans reflect Ethan's keen desire to see the world beyond the Berkshires and to make his own contribution to it.

The crippled figure whom the narrator meets more than twenty years later never experienced that world, for naturalism is the chronicle of unfulfilled lives. The newlywed's plans to sell his property were soon thwarted by the onset of his wife's different maladies, and he had no choice but to remain in the village which he had outgrown. Dreaming of invigorating new surroundings when he married, Ethan instead found himself yoked more tightly to a failing farm on the outskirts of Starkfield. The constricting nature of this environment is clear to the narrator before he ever enters the Frome kitchen. The depleted farm which he views on his ride to Corbury Junction presents itself unmistakably as one of the obstacles which barred the younger Ethan's flight. Viewing the "exanimate" saw-mill and the "starved" apple trees in the orchard, the narrator is dismayed. Continuing past the shabby farmhouse framed by snow, he is rendered speechless by "the distress and oppression of the scene" (71). The forlorn house is lacking its "L," that New England annex designed to connect a home with a barn or shed nearby. Ethan tersely explains that he was obliged to dismantle the "L" some time ago, and the narrator finds the loss of this familiar structure symbolic. Like Thoreau by his cabin at Walden or Jay Gatsby in his Long Island mansion, Ethan Frome is identified by his home. The "diminished dwelling" where he lives with Zeena and Mattie is the "image of his own shrunken body," the projection of the failure which he has experienced in Starkfield (72).

This stricken house thus reveals Ethan to the narrator as no villager ever could. Tantalized by Harmon Gow and rebuffed by Mrs. Hale in his efforts to know more about Ethan, the visiting engineer has only unanswered questions when he takes refuge at the farm during a blizzard. Once he crosses the threshold of the cramped, cold farmhouse, however, he gains the "clue" he needs to begin his narrative of Ethan's broken life. He first perceived the house as "one of those lonely New England farm-houses that make the landscape lonelier" (71), and he finds nothing in the life which he observes there to suggest that the façade is misleading. When Ethan arrives home on this night, hours later than expected because of the dangerous storm raging outside, neither woman seated in the kitchen greets him or acknowledges the stranger with him. The room itself is poor and barren, stripped of all but a few pieces of shabby furniture and enough rough china for the three who live together. When the men enter, one woman rises wordlessly to fetch the remnants of a cold pie and the other begins a fresh complaint about the temperature in the room. Through these spare details, Wharton characterizes Ethan's home as a place lacking the nourishment and warmth which he needs. Her narrator sees enough in this space to fashion his "vision" of Ethan Frome as a figure who lives apart and moves in a silence which he cannot escape.

The story inspired by this visit to the Frome farmhouse is the narrator's recreation of the events surrounding the "smash up." This short narrative is acutely psychological, focusing on a younger Ethan yearning for a more satisfying life than the one he knows as Zeena's husband. The first three chapters of the novel establish his attraction to Mattie, the source of his rekindled desire to escape his struggling farm and unhappy marriage. His wife's overnight trip to consult a new doctor in Bettsbridge precipitates the novel's crisis, in part because it seems to confirm how much happier he would be if he could free himself of this sickly, discontented woman who seldom speaks. Observing Zeena in the kitchen on the morning of her unexpected leave taking, Ethan sees only the disparity between their ages and their fundamental incompatibility: "She sat opposite the window, and the pale light reflected from the banks of snow made her face look more than usually drawn and bloodless, sharpened the three parallel creases between ear and cheek, and drew querulous lines from her thin nose to the corners of her mouth. Though she was but seven years her husband's senior, and he was only twenty-eight, she was already an old woman" (95). The contrast which he perceives between Zeena and Mattie preoccupies him more deeply, for the latter offers him understanding and conversation missing from his life for too many years.

Zeena's short trip provides Ethan with the opportunity to experience a measure of the life that he craves. He finds that his surroundings are transformed as soon as Zeena leaves for the train; her absence is all that is required to restore "a homelike look" and feeling to the house (96). Under Mattie's influence, the kitchen exudes a sunny warmth and vitality that lift his spirits and fan the "slumbering spark of sociability" (96) dormant since he left Worcester. He completes his day's errands and chores with élan, eager to claim his evening alone with Mattie. Yet his return home is punctuated by the sight of a familiar tombstone in the family graveyard commemorating the peaceful marriage of a couple who were together fifty years, Ethan and his wife Endurance. Filled with thoughts of Mattie, he finds himself wondering ironically if a similar headstone will one day mark the grave of Ethan and Zeena. Hemmed in by circumstances he cannot seem to change, he is reminded of how quickly fifty years of his life may pass. This experience of memento mori furthers the novel's ongoing characterization of Ethan Frome as someone more dead than alive (see Chapter 5), and it also supplies a valuable context for the evening he spends imagining that Mattie rather than Zeena is his wife.

Zeena's return the next afternoon ends more than Ethan's private fantasies about the married life he might have known with Mattie. The new doctor's diagnosis—that Zeena suffers from "complications," not merely "troubles"—has filled her with fresh purpose and determination (118). Knowing that "complications" invariably lead to death, Ethan is initially torn between sympathy for his sick wife and hope for his own release. However, her announcement that she needs more help in the house and has already hired a young woman inflames Ethan with anger. He makes no headway in the bitter argument which ensues, for Zeena's notion of conciliation is to remind him that they will soon be spared the expense of boarding Mattie any longer. He can only listen in horror to Zeena's plan to replace the woman he loves with a hired girl from Bettsbridge, for Mattie is her poor relation and not his. As he tries desperately to appeal to his wife's conscience, she silences him by alluding to village gossip about Mattie's continuing presence in their home. These words of Zeena's strike him with the force of "a knife-cut across the sinews," and he is rendered helpless (123). When he learns that she intends to send Mattie away the next day, Ethan also recognizes the depth of his own hatred and frustration.

Ethan looked at her with loathing. . . . It was the sense of his helplessness that sharpened his antipathy. There had never been anything in her that one could appeal to; but as long as he could ignore and command he had remained indifferent. Now she had mastered him and he abhorred her. . . . All the long misery of his baffled past, of his youth of failure, hardship and vain effort, rose up in his soul in bitterness and seemed to take shape before him in the woman who at every turn barred his way. She had taken everything else from him; and now she meant to take the one thing that made up for all the others. For a moment such a flame of hate rose in him that it ran down his arm and clenched his fist against her. He took a wild step forward and then stopped. (123–24)

As Ethan faces the loss of Mattie, Zeena appears to be something worse than an obstacle blocking his path. He now views their marriage as a relationship based on power, one in which he can neither "command" nor "master" his wife. All too aware of his helplessness, he checks his impulse to violence and asks in some confusion whether she will be eating dinner that evening.

In a pattern familiar to American naturalism, Ethan's knowledge of his own powerlessness guides the remaining action of the novel. Cowed by the defeat he has suffered in the room he shares reluctantly with Zeena, he fares no better when he attempts to protect Mattie by claiming that the cat broke Aunt Philura Maple's red pickle dish. Incensed by the discovery of the broken wedding gift, Zeena denounces Mattie savagely and makes clear that the younger woman's return to Stamford is inevitable. Ethan spends the night that follows in deepening confusion in his self-styled study, unwilling to take his accustomed place by Zeena in their bedroom. The unheated space becomes a fitting setting for his deliberations, for this retreat effectively embodies his squandered prospects. Contemplating what his marriage has become, he chafes at the waste of his best energies and ambition: "He was too young, too strong, too full of the sap of living, to submit so easily to the destruction of his hopes. Must he wear out all his years at the side of a bitter querulous woman? Other possibilities had been in him, possibilities sacrificed, one by one, to Zeena's narrow-mindedness and ignorance. And what good had come of it?" (129–30). Ethan is tormented increasingly by these questions which he cannot answer. His frustration illuminates a common theme of naturalistic novels, a theme which Pizer describes as "the waste of individual potential because of the conditioning forces of life" (20).

Inevitably then, Ethan's attempts to overcome these forces are doomed. Alone in his study, he decides that he and Mattie should escape to the West and pursue the success that a different Berkshire farmer achieved only a few years earlier when he divorced his wife for another woman. Ethan is charmed by the memory of this couple's recent visit home to Shadd's Falls, accompanied by a cherubic daughter "dressed like a princess" (130). This archetypal American dream of starting over founders quickly, however, as Ethan is forced to acknowledge how completely he is trapped in Starkfield. The farm and mill are already heavily mortgaged, so he has nothing to leave Zeena and no means of even paying for the train tickets he and Mattie will require for their new life together. "The inexorable facts closed in on him like prison-warders hand-cuffing a convict. There was no way out—none. He was a prisoner for life, and now his one ray of light was to be extinguished" (131). Wharton's vivid imagery reinforces the novel's strain of determinism, portraying Ethan at this late juncture as a captive denied any possibility of escape from the circumstances of his life.

Throughout Chapters VIII and IX, Ethan struggles ineffectually against his bonds. He dwells on the two painful truths that Mattie has nowhere to go when she leaves his farm and that he can do nothing to rescue her. Watching his neighbor depart for the station with Mattie's trunk, he himself feels he is in the grip of forces beyond his control: "It seemed to Ethan that his heart was bound with cords which an unseen hand was tightening with every tick of the clock" (138). He resents his role of "helpless spectator at Mattie's banishment" (134) and repeatedly assures her that he would take decisive steps on her behalf if he could.[6] During his impromptu outing to Shadow Pond with Mattie, he savors the illusion that he is a free man enjoying a date with his fiancée. More characteristically, he repeatedly assures her that he would leave with her—would do *something*—if he were only able to act. The refrain is persistent: " 'You know there's nothing I wouldn't do for you if I could,' " he tells her; " 'Oh, Matt . . . if I could ha' gone with you now I'd ha' done it,' " he protests (143). As darkness falls, he grows more plaintive about the limitations on his freedom: " 'I'm tied hand and foot, Matt. There isn't a thing I can do' " (144). He repeats this sentiment at the moment that the two reach the crest of School House Hill, exclaiming that he cannot " 'lift a hand' " to keep Mattie with him. Following their final run down the same hill into the big elm tree, Ethan's helplessness increases dramatically when he awakens after the crash and feels trapped beneath "a rock, or some huge mass" (151).

The closing pages of the novel, set twenty-four years after this abortive suicide attempt, make clear that Ethan never succeeded in removing the obstacles barring his flight from Starkfield. One of Wharton's fullest explorations of naturalism, *Ethan Frome* depicts its protagonist as a man whose choices have been limited sharply by circumstance. Yet Wharton is distinguished from contemporary naturalistic writers by her refusal to deny characters such as Ethan moral responsibility for their actions. Like Stephen Crane, she establishes the often oppressive influence of environment but insists that it influences—rather than determines—the choices her characters make. Carol Singley comments on the importance of this distinction: "Naturalists underplay individual choices and power; Wharton, however, although acknowledging limitations, gives her characters some measure of moral freedom. Naturalists logically hold that no one is to blame in a world subject to natural laws; Wharton makes her characters morally accountable, even if they are not morally aware" (64). Despite the restrictions placed on him, Ethan Frome retains his free will to the moment of his descent down School House Hill. He is responsible for the pivotal decision which he makes near the close of Chapter VIII, for example, when he will not secure his escape (and Mattie's) by betraying the trust of the compassionate Hales. Midway through his encounter with Mrs. Hale, he chooses not to proceed with his plan to lie to her husband so that he can buy the train tickets he needs. In desperate circumstances, only hours before Mattie leaves him, he is capable of judgment and right action: "With the sudden perception of the point to which his madness had carried him, the madness fell and he saw his life before him as it was. He was a poor man, the husband of a sickly woman, whom his desertion would leave alone and destitute; and even if he had the heart to desert her he could have done so only by deceiving two kindly people who had pitied him" (136). By refusing to dupe the Hales, Ethan sacrifices his last hope for a life with Mattie outside the confines of Starkfield. Leaving Mrs. Hale, he directs his slow step back to the farm and to the responsibilities awaiting him there.

The narrator's re-creation of the life which Ethan has known since that day closes the novel. The visiting engineer frustrated about his ability to penetrate

the "deeper meaning" of Ethan's story (65) sees more than enough on the
night of the storm to complete his narrative. What he learns is that the young
farmer who was once frantic to keep Mattie by his side has spent decades on a
remote farm with her and his wife, in one of the bleaker romantic triangles of
American fiction. The harshness of the three figures' lives together in the
stricken farmhouse expresses both the "hard compulsions of the poor" (155)
and the prevailing hopelessness of so many contemporary works of naturalism. The fate which Wharton imagines for her most famous protagonist
seems to bear out Norris' claim that "terrible things must happen to the
characters of the naturalistic tale." At an even more important level, the story
of Ethan Frome reveals the inevitability of suffering in her most representative fiction.[7] The painful isolation which he experiences afflicts one major
Wharton character after another, from Lily Bart in *The House of Mirth* (1905)
to Martin Boyne of *The Children* (1928). An emblematic novel, *Ethan Frome*
looks unflinchingly at a life shaped by irremediable loneliness and loss.

THE HABIT OF SPECTATORSHIP

The House of Mirth begins in a train station on a hot afternoon in early
September, as the wellborn Lawrence Selden savors the unexpected sight of
the lovely Lily Bart. The opening chapter of this novel characterizes Selden as
a figure who enjoys watching Lily and speculating about her intentions,
despite the fact that they have known each other for many years. With her
deft irony, Wharton relies on passive voice construction to define the nature
of Selden's interest in Lily from his first glimpse of her. "In the afternoon
rush of the Grand Central Station his eyes had been refreshed by the sight of
Miss Lily Bart" (3). The narration that follows relies on verbs of vision and
language of conjecture to identify Selden as a man who prefers observation to
action. Surprised to find Lily in town at this point in the season, he indulges
in the pleasure of studying her from a distance and debating her motives
rather than greeting her. "There was nothing new about Lily Bart, yet he
could never see her without a faint movement of interest: it was characteristic
of her that she always roused speculation, that her simplest acts seemed the
result of far-reaching intentions" (3). To amuse himself further, Selden decides to test Lily by placing himself in her path without appearing to see her.
A spectator in her life to the end of the novel, he protects himself against her
sheer attractiveness by making her responsible for any contact between them.

This figure of the passive spectator recurs in Wharton's fiction, resulting in
a group of intellectual or artistic male protagonists defined largely by their
interiority.[8] Wharton traces the implications of this habit of spectatorship in
The House of Mirth, portraying the cultivated Selden as a figure unwilling
to sacrifice his ironic detachment even to gain the fuller life he desires.
She continues to develop this theme in the later *Ethan Frome*, thus supplying
another potent reason for her title character's failure to act decisively.

An unlikely counterpart to the lawyer Selden, her beleaguered young farmer is an intellectual in spite of his interrupted college education. Torn between his duty to Zeena and his passion for Mattie, Ethan spends much of the novel in solitary thought as he tries (vainly) to overcome his deepening confusion. Through her depiction of his internal struggle, Wharton criticizes that habit of spectatorship which leads to paralysis of the will.

   The first two chapters of *Ethan Frome* introduce the protagonist as a figure dangerously preoccupied with watching Mattie at a safe remove. The action of the novel begins with Ethan alone, deep in thought, on his way to the church dance in Starkfield. Eager for conversation with her on the two-mile walk back to the farm, he nonetheless fails to enter the brightly lighted church when he reaches it. Instead of joining the assembled company of neighbors and friends in the basement, he positions himself near a window where he cannot be seen.

The young man, skirting the side of the building, went down the slope toward the basement door. To keep out of range of the revealing rays from within he made a circuit through the untrodden snow and gradually approached the farther angle of the basement wall. Thence, still hugging the shadow, he edged his way cautiously forward to the nearest window, holding back his straight spare body and craning his neck till he got a glimpse of the room. (76)

The language and tone of this passage emphasize the furtiveness of Ethan's movements as he chooses his vantage point. More intent on observing Mattie than meeting her, he remains the "hidden watcher" (84) for the remainder of the dance. In the process, he consigns himself to a lonely vigil in the cold night air while fellow villagers enjoy the warmth and light and music of the final dances of the evening.

   Ethan's motive for spying becomes clearer once he locates Mattie in the room. From his dark post, he watches as she happily leads a Virginia reel with Denis Eady, the grocer's son whom he regards as rival. Ethan's jealousy intensifies quickly as he notes the gaiety of Mattie in motion, "her laughing panting lips, the cloud of dark hair about her forehead, and the dark eyes which seemed the only fixed points in a maze of flying lines" (77). Unwilling to join the dance, he dwells on the violence which he would like to visit on Eady. Ethan's resentment deepens as he broods over the way Mattie reveals her pleasure in the spontaneity of the moment. "He even noticed two or three gestures which, in his fatuity, he had thought she kept for him: a way of throwing her head back when she was amused, as if to taste her laugh before she let it out, and a trick of sinking her lids slowly when anything charmed or moved her" (79–80). Convincing himself that the woman he loves but cannot court has given her affection to another, Ethan decides to test her when the dance draws to a close. He remains hidden from view as the villagers drift away from the church, intent on learning whether Mattie will accept Eady's offer to drive her back to the farm in his cutter. Ethan waits anxiously as she scans the darkness for him, and he strains to hear her exchanges with Eady. Only after Mattie refuses Eady's offer a second time—and begins walking alone in the darkness—does Ethan make his presence known to her. Although she treats Ethan's eavesdropping as a mischievous game, Wharton characterizes his silent watching outside the church as part of a more insidious pattern within the novel.

The nature of Ethan's thoughts while he waits for Mattie illuminates another striking aspect of his passivity. An introspective figure who has endured years of silence with his ill mother and then his hypochondriac wife, he is accustomed to dreaming about the life he cannot have. Through-out the novel, he is inclined to retreat from the conditions of his life on the farm into reveries about nature or private fantasies about Mattie. His discovery that she shares his appreciation for the beauty of the Berkshires has inspired him to new flights of the imagination, for he believes that he has found someone capable of expressing his "secret soul" (79). Increasingly absorbed in daydreams about Mattie, he thinks confidently—and unrealisti-cally—of the instant improvements which she will make in her housekeeping as soon as she marries the right person. "She was quick to learn, but forgetful and dreamy, and not disposed to take the matter [of housekeeping] seriously. Ethan had an idea that if she were to marry a man she was fond of the dormant instinct would wake, and her pies and biscuits become the pride of the county; but domesticity in the abstract did not interest her" (80). Wharton's ironic tone underscores the contrast between one who is governed by ideas and the other who eschews abstractions. Ethan has been secretly completing as many of Mattie's chores as he can, yet he holds fast to the idea that she is capable of running an exceptional home.

Even more telling is Ethan's reaction to the sight of the family graveyard as he returns home with Mattie. For years he has perceived the gravestones within as mute reproaches to his ambitions for a life beyond Starkfield. Help-less to escape the farm, he has felt mocked by the reminders of so many other Fromes who passed their lives within the bounds of the property. With Mattie at his side, however, he suddenly finds in these same gravestones a tangible promise of continuity. The gap between what he says to her and what he thinks extends the novel's portrayal of him as a spectator. He murmurs to her, "'I guess we'll never let you go, Matt,'" but he tells himself, "We'll always go on living here together, and some day she'll lie there beside me" (88). Unwilling to speak the last words directly to her, he instead lingers privately over his vision of their life together.

He let the vision possess him as they climbed the hill to the house. He was never so happy with her as when he abandoned himself to these dreams. Half-way up the slope Mattie stumbled against some unseen obstruction and clutched his sleeve to steady herself. The wave of warmth that went through him was like the prolongation of his vision. For the first time he stole his arm about her, and she did not resist. (88)

The relation between dream and reality is a complicated one for Ethan, who delights in Mattie's presence chiefly because it sustains and enriches his vision of her. Lost in his romantic reverie, he enjoys his first physical contact with her only when she reaches unexpectedly for him.

During his evening alone in the farmhouse with Mattie, Ethan comes no closer to acting decisively on his feelings. The emphasis of Chapters IV and V falls instead on his observations and his illusions. He perceives the center of the house, the kitchen, in a new, warmer light as soon as Mattie assumes Zeena's place in it. Caught up in thoughts of a winter night by the fire with Mattie, he races through the day's chores. As he works, he embellishes his vision of the hours he will share with her: "For the first time they would be alone together indoors, and they would sit there, one on each side of the stove, like a married couple, he in his stocking feet and smoking his pipe, she laughing and talking in that funny way she had, which was always as new to him as if he had never heard her before" (96). Relishing this tableau, Ethan expresses himself in a rare outburst of singing on his way to the village. Inspired by "the sweetness of the picture" in his mind, he anticipates that the night ahead will dispel the shades of cold and silence which he has endured since he left Worcester (96).

Yet Wharton demonstrates the fragility of Ethan's fantasies in several pointed ways, even before his evening with Mattie begins. His vision of Mattie and himself together by the fire, "like a married couple," is easily supplanted by more sobering images in the village. The mere sight of Denis Eady in his cutter changes Ethan's mood abruptly. Overtaken by jealousy once again, he decides that Eady has learned of Zeena's absence and is leaving the village to woo Mattie while the farmhouse is empty. An encounter under the black Varnum spruces by the church, where Ethan and Mattie stood together only the night before, is nearly as disconcerting. Savoring the memory of his closeness to Mattie in this spot, he is initially amused to see Ned Hale and Ruth Varnum kissing in the shadows. As the two figures separate in embarrassment at his approach, however, Ethan is struck by the difference between their circumstances and his. Ned and Ruth are engaged to be married soon, but Ethan can only fantasize about his own union with Mattie.

Mattie's dramatic appearance at the kitchen door seems to restore Ethan's sense of possibility. Smiling on the spot where a dour Zeena stood only the night before, Mattie appears radiant to him, "taller, fuller, more womanly in shape and motion" (103). Seeing the festive table she has set for their meal together, he is filled with quiet satisfaction. The specter of Eady has been banished, and Ethan is determined to suppress thoughts of Zeena. Taking his place by the fire after completing his evening's chores, he is confident that the evening ahead will fulfill his expectations: "The scene was just as he had dreamed of it that morning. He sat down, drew his pipe from his pocket and stretched his feet to the glow. His hard day's work in the keen air made him feel at once lazy and light of mood, and he had a confused sense of being in another world, where all was warmth and harmony and time could bring no change" (107). This other world does not exist, of course, and Wharton directs potent irony against Ethan as he retreats from life into the illusions that he has generated. When he directs Mattie to draw closer and sit in the chair where Zeena usually rocks, he is rewarded by the vision of his wife's face replacing that of the "intruder" (107). When he attempts to move his own chair to see Mattie more closely, Zeena's cat leaps into the empty rocking chair and stands watch over the two of them.[9] He fails each time that he attempts to adapt reality to the picture in his mind, and he cannot shake off reminders of Zeena however hard he tries to pretend that Mattie is his spouse.

Content nonetheless to observe Mattie and dream of the relationship which they could have in "another world," Ethan passes his evening alone with her without ever touching her. Jarred by the sudden recognition that Zeena will be in her usual place again the next night, he reaches out for Mattie and grasps the cloth she is sewing instead. The way he fondles and eventually kisses this material emphasizes the unbroken distance between them. The long evening ends soon after, with Ethan watching Mattie close her bedroom door for the night and recalling that he has not even touched her hand. Yet that omission seems unimportant to him the next morning, as he eats his breakfast and hoards his private joy.

He did not know why he was so irrationally happy, for nothing was changed in his life or hers. He had not even touched the tip of her fingers or looked her full in the eyes. But their evening together had given him a vision of what life at her side might be, and he was glad now that he had done nothing to trouble the sweetness of the picture. He had a fancy that she knew what had restrained him. (113)

Here and elsewhere, protecting his vision of life with Mattie means remaining apart from her in a reality of his own. His sense that he need not explain himself to her is unfounded, as Wharton demonstrates in Chapter VII when he embraces Mattie immediately following his defeat at Zeena's hands. Unaware of his thoughts—or his feelings—Mattie learns of her fate only after he kisses her to ease his own pain. "She lingered a moment, caught in the same strong current; then she slipped from him and drew back a step or two, pale and troubled. Her look smote him with compunction, and he cried out, as if he saw her drowning in a dream: 'You can't go, Matt! I'll never let you!'" (124). Even in this moment of intimacy, he perceives her through the filter of a dream. His vow to protect her proves as insubstantial as his visions, for he remains a "helpless spectator at Mattie's banishment" to the novel's climax on School House Hill.

Long after she completed the story of Ethan Frome, Wharton continued to explore imaginatively the moral consequences of spectatorship. Her comic masterpiece *The Custom of the Country*, published only two years after *Ethan Frome*, furthers her critique of the sensitive male character incapable of active engagement with life. A husband of the rapacious Undine Spragg of Apex City, Ralph Marvell is the scion of a fading but distinguished family of Old New York. Smitten with the beautiful Undine despite her vulgarity, he chooses to view her as a mythological figure in need of rescue: "He seemed to see her—as he sat there, pressing his fists into his temples—he seemed to see her like a lovely rock-bound Andromeda, with the devouring monster Society careering up to make a mouthful of her; and himself whirling down on his winged horse—just Pegasus turned Rosinante for the nonce—to cut her bonds, snatch her up, and whirl her back into the blue" (*Novels* 676–77). The extravagance of the conceit reveals Ralph's characteristic idealism, for he aspires to a life with Undine on some ethereal plane far from the world in which he moves. He marries her without ever recognizing the intensity of her desire to enter—and dominate—that society which he dreams of escaping. Unable to match her restless energy or curb her impetuous behavior, Ralph responds by retreating deeper and deeper into an inner world imaged as a secret cave which no one may enter (*Novels* 672). Divorced from Undine and unable to retain custody of their son Paul, he eventually withdraws from the struggle altogether by committing suicide. In Ralph Marvell's choice of death over life, Wharton again exposes the vulnerability of a figure defined by his passivity.

A NARROW RANGE OF POSSIBILITIES FOR WOMEN

Although the novel focuses most closely on the blighted life of Ethan Frome, it also illuminates the unsatisfactory circumstances of the two women trapped with him in a dilapidated farmhouse. In Mattie Silver's predicament, Wharton expresses her strongest and most familiar criticism of the limitations placed on women in nineteenth-century American society. An attractive young woman who has been recently orphaned, Mattie has few prospects for an independent existence outside marriage. Her growing desperation to remain on the farm thus reflects more than her romantic attraction to Ethan, as she is all too aware that she cannot support herself in the modern city. The motives of Mattie's antagonist are also important to this theme, for Wharton portrays Zeena as a woman damaged by the isolation and frustration of her days on a remote farm. The "queerness" which Zeena is beginning to exhibit is so widespread that it functions in the novel as an indictment of the lonely conditions of life in the Berkshires. In this regard, Wharton's characterization is shaped by her perception of the region's villages as "grim places, morally and physically"—as impoverished communities harboring "insanity, incest and slow mental and moral starvation" behind unpainted façades (*Backward Glance* 294). Within *Ethan Frome*, the intertwined fates of Zeena and Mattie dramatize the constricting effect of such a setting.[10]

The two women begin the novel in strikingly different positions. Younger and more vibrant than Zeena, Mattie entered Starkfield a year earlier as a waif unable to provide for herself in the city. She arrived at the train station a "colourless slip of a thing," so frail from her recent months of work in Stamford that Ethan could not imagine how she would be able to help Zeena with household chores (91). A year on the farm has since restored her health and vigor, but she remains entirely dependent on the dour Zeena for her board. Mattie's first conversation with Ethan in the novel (Chapter II) captures vividly her fear of losing the only home left to her. Returning to the farm together after the church dance in the village, they talk merrily of the sledding that occurs on School House Hill throughout the winter and make their own plans to coast the following night. Discomfited by her claim of fearlessness and her sudden show of independence when she walks on without him, he upsets her much more than he intended to when he raises the question of her leaving the Fromes. His idle reference to village gossip about her future changes the tenor of the conversation abruptly, for she leaps to the painful conclusion that Zeena has decided to send her away. Selfishly absorbed in extracting the assurance that Mattie will not marry Denis Eady, he fails to consider the fundamental insecurity of her life. Her reaction to his heedless words underscores how fearful and dependent she actually is. His confidence restored when he learns that she has no intention of leaving the farm, he ignores her poignant question, "Where'd I go, if I did [leave]?" (88).

Wharton uses this exchange to introduce Mattie as an acutely vulnerable figure. The exposition that follows in Chapter III supplies the reasons for her plight in the form of recent family history. The daughter of a cousin of Zeena's, Mattie was raised for a life more genteel than that of "indentured" servant on a hardscrabble farm (92). Her father Orin Silver was a prominent businessman in Stamford, building ambitiously on the reputation and fortune of his wife's father. After her father's unexpected death, however, Mattie and her mother were forced to confront both the shoddy nature of his business practices and the reality of their poverty. Unable to survive these discoveries, Mattie's mother died soon after her husband. Mattie became an orphan at the age of twenty and resorted to selling her piano to raise fifty dollars for her keep. She learned quickly that family would not rally to her aid in these circumstances, for too many of her relatives suffered the loss of their savings when they trusted her father to make lucrative investments on their behalf. Alone for the first time in her life, Mattie struggled vainly to take her place in the modern work force: "When she tried to extend the field of her activities in the direction of stenography and book-keeping her health broke down, and six months on her feet behind the counter of a department store did not tend to restore it" (92). Worn down by these efforts to support herself, Mattie had no choice but to accept Zeena's offer to live on the farm and work as an unpaid servant in the household. Mattie's claims on this position remain tenuous a year later, for she lacks all but the most rudimentary ability to clean and cook.

In several important ways, the novel emphasizes how unprepared Mattie is for any sort of independent existence. Her failures outside the home (stenography, accounting, shop keeping) are hardly redeemed by her performance inside the home, where Ethan routinely completes as many of her chores as he can in an effort to disguise her "unskilled efforts" (80). Knowing that Mattie has neither natural aptitude nor training for the housework required of her, he fetches wood, washes floors and even churns butter. As Zeena becomes more vocal in her dissatisfaction, Mattie's situation grows more precarious. Wharton's criticism of the larger society's expectations for women emerges in the novel's repeated references to Mattie as unskilled, inefficient and weak. Wharton directs particularly strong irony against the training which Mattie did receive, exposing the paucity of her talents merely by listing them: "For this purpose [of making her way in the world] her equipment, though varied, was inadequate. She could trim a hat, make molasses candy, recite 'Curfew shall not ring to-night,' and play 'The Lost Chord' and a pot-pourri from 'Carmen'" (92). Mattie's slim accomplishments are distinctly genteel in nature, intended to charm a husband rather than impress an employer or maintain a household.

In the nature of her upbringing and the narrowness of her prospects, Mattie Silver is a recognizable Wharton character. Preoccupied by the lack of viable choices for women in modern American society, Wharton created one doomed protagonist after another in the novels *The House of Mirth* (1905), *The Fruit of the Tree* (1907), *Ethan Frome* (1911) and *The Reef* (1912).[11] The pattern is set memorably in *The House of Mirth*, the novel which places the stunning Lily Bart at the mercy of a glittering, false society. Less imposing than Lily, Mattie is nonetheless a successor of hers, for both characters are orphans without loving family or material resources at their disposal. The parallels extend to the treatment each receives from relations intent on nursing grievances from the past (Mrs. Bart's snobbery in *House of Mirth*, Mr. Silver's theft in *Ethan Frome*). Mrs. Peniston, Lily's reluctant guardian, assumes responsibility for her grieving eighteen-year-old niece with the words, " 'I'll try her for a year' " (37). Mattie encounters even greater indifference to her plight, until relatives seize the opportunity to make the daughter pay for the father's crimes by sending her to the Frome farm. Zeena's decision in Chapter VII to replace Mattie with a hired girl is announced in dismissive language worthy of Mrs. Peniston: " 'She's a pauper that's hung onto us all after her father'd done his best to ruin us. I've kep' her a whole year: it's somebody else's turn now' " (122). When Lily falls from favor with Mrs. Peniston, she fares no better in the workroom of Madame Regina's millinery shop than Mattie in the Stamford store. When Mattie is banished from the farmhouse, she prefers death to the life awaiting her in the shops and factories of the Northeast.[12]

Late in *The House of Mirth*, Lily considers her own limitations and the reason for them. Her sense of herself as merely decorative bears directly on Wharton's characterization of Mattie: "Since she had been brought up to be ornamental, she could hardly blame herself for failing to serve any practical purpose" (*House of Mirth* 313). The two novels argue that the "purpose" reserved for young women at the end of the nineteenth century is marriage. Surveying the disparate settings of Old New York and a Berkshire village, Wharton is criticizing the assumptions of American society as a whole. Lily acknowledges her purpose in her first encounter with Selden, even as she covets his small apartment and expresses her desire for a flat of her own. She lacks the ability even to imagine a satisfying independent existence for herself, for she was raised to marry a suitably wealthy husband and preside over her own country house. Her fashionable society affords her no examples of women who have achieved such an existence, a point Wharton emphasizes each time Gerty Farish or Carrie Fisher appears in the novel. Perceiving the impossibility of holding his cousin Gerty out to Lily as a model, Selden contemplates his guest's inevitable function: "As he watched her hand, polished as a bit of old ivory, with its slender pink nails, and the sapphire bracelet slipping over her wrist, he was struck with the irony of suggesting to her such a life as his cousin Gertrude Farish had chosen. She was so evidently the victim of the civilization which had produced her, that the links of her bracelet seemed like manacles chaining her to her fate" (7). He listens willingly enough as Lily frets about friends who say that she should have married by now, but responds more bluntly than she expects: " 'Isn't marriage your vocation? Isn't it what you're all brought up for?' " (9). Lily's reply echoes ironically through more than one Wharton novel, for she sighs and agrees, " 'I suppose so. What else is there?' " (9).

Mattie Silver can find no better answer to this question than Lily. Confined to a remote farm for much of her year in Starkfield, Zeena's poor relation is expected to marry the grocer's son. The first scene of the novel identifies him as her most promising suitor, with Ethan resenting what he perceives as Denis Eady's "almost impudent ownership" of her (77) and Zeena irritable about the hired girl she will need to find when the marriage occurs. Mattie's impoverished circumstances make her vocation patently obvious to the Fromes and their neighbors, for she can neither return to her father's house nor attempt another job in the city. The courtship between Denis and Mattie never materializes, of course, for she wants only to continue living at the farm as an unpaid servant in order to remain close to Ethan.[13]

When Mattie learns that she must leave Starkfield, she insists more and more forcefully that she cannot survive on her own. At the novel's climax, as she presses Ethan to kill them both at the foot of the icy hill, she reveals the depth of her need in poignant language: " 'Ethan, where'll I go if I leave you? I don't know how to get along alone' " (148). Her unwillingness to begin a life apart from him is expressed here as a failure of knowledge or preparation. Characterized for most of the novel as someone with no home or fixed identity of her own, Mattie would rather die than continue alone. As Elizabeth Ammons suggests, Mattie's choice at twilight has consequences which advance the novel's theme: "The fact that Wharton cripples Mattie, but will not let her die, reflects not the author's but the culture's cruelty. Like Lily Bart at the opposite end of the social scale, Mattie Silver has not been prepared for an economically independent life. The system is designed to keep her a parasite or a drudge, or both" (152–53). Denied the death which she sought, she is trapped on an isolated farm for the next twenty-four years. Once afraid to leave Ethan, she spends her days in bitterly close proximity to him *and* his wife. Paralyzed in her chair, she exemplifies the constricted life available within the world of the novel.

Wharton's criticism of women's roles also influences her characterization of Zeena, a married figure no more fulfilled than unmarried Mattie. Although Ethan's wife is not a center of interest for *Ethan Frome*, her circumstances are representative of a larger nineteenth-century problem. Named for the magnificent Zenobia of Hawthorne's *The Blithedale Romance*, Zeena Frome has none of her fictional predecessor's achievements and only her illness to distinguish her. Isolated on the Frome farm, she derives her identify from her status as an invalid requiring more and more care and attention. She achieved this status only a year after she married Ethan, cultivating the " 'sickliness' which had since made her notable even in a community rich in pathological instances" (98). As a woman suffering from a host of unnamed problems—including neurasthenia and hypochondria—she is associated with the nineteenth-century phenomenon of hysteria (Smith-Rosenberg 197). Coping with an invalid spouse herself and thoroughly familiar with the treatment methods of the leading specialist S. Weir Mitchell, Wharton defines Zeena in terms of her sickliness and its effect on the household.

Zeena is associated with nineteenth-century patent medicines and medical visits from the novel's earliest references to her. In the prologue, the narrator sees her disfigured husband collecting mail for her more than once. None of the correspondence interests Frome, but the narrator notes that the envelopes addressed to "Mrs. Zenobia Frome" bear return addresses from makers of various patent medicines. When Zeena appears for the first time in the novel proper (Chapter III), her opening remark is a complaint about her health. Materializing suddenly at the door of the farmhouse as Ethan searches vainly for the key, she is a composite of angularity and odd shadows (particularly in contrast to the glowing Mattie). Her sleeplessness is due to illness; she explains, " 'I just felt so mean I couldn't sleep' " (90). When Ethan returns from the fields for breakfast the next morning, he finds his wife dressed for travel with his valise at her side. Having learned of a new doctor to consult about her worsening "shooting pains," she has unexpectedly decided to take an overnight trip to Bettsbridge (94). These trips are usually associated with expenses the farm cannot absorb—such as the $20 electrical battery which she has never mastered—but Ethan reflects that his wife is a person "wholly absorbed in her health" (94). Seated by the window in the winter sunlight, she appears to him an old woman already despite the fact that she is only thirty-five (seven years his senior).

Zeena's dramatic return from her visit to Dr. Buck is the catalyst for much of the action which follows. When Ethan finds her in their darkening bedroom, refusing supper because she is too sick to eat, he expects their conversation to follow the "consecrated formula" in which she eventually changes out of her traveling clothes and accompanies him downstairs to the table (118). She is accustomed to holding her husband's attention through reminders of her poor health, and her physical symptoms form the only subject which interests her. She collects medical opinions from doctors, relatives and neighbors; she doses herself with quantities of various patent medicines before bed and after meals; and she reads a book entitled *Kidney Troubles and Their Cure* at the breakfast table. Historian Caroll Smith-Rosenberg describes a similar pattern in her work *Disorderly Conduct: Visions of Gender in Victorian America*:

Because medical wisdom had defined hysteria as a disease, its victims could expect to be treated as sick and thus to elicit a particular set of responses—the right to be seen and treated by a physician, to stay in bed and thus be relieved of their normal day-to-day responsibilities, to enjoy the special prerogatives, indulgences, and sympathy the sick role entailed. Hysteria thus became one way in which conventional women could express—in most cases unconsciously—dissatisfaction with one or several aspects of their lives. (208)

Buoyed by her visit to a new doctor, Zeena informs Ethan that she is sicker than he realizes and thus in need of much more help in the house. Her condition now requires the presence of a bona fide hired girl, one who will discharge all household tasks more reliably than Mattie has done. With the demeanor of someone "consciously singled out for a great fate," Zeena tells Ethan that her health has deteriorated further. She went to Bettsbridge afflicted with "troubles," but she has returned (triumphantly) with "complications" (118).

That diagnosis appears to give Zeena even greater authority in her home, for she maintains her dominance in the household through her claims of infirmity. Mattie struggles at her chores in constant fear of displeasing Zeena; Ethan works long hours on a failing farm without ever questioning the exact nature of his wife's maladies. As Marlene Springer suggests, illness is the source of power as well as identity for Ethan's wife (*Nightmare of Need* 65). This aspect of Zeena's character is particularly apparent in

Chapter VII, as she and Ethan wage the first open battle of their marriage. Reacting in anger to the news that Zeena has hired a servant to live on the farm, Ethan recognizes that her development of "complications" is a deliberate strategy designed to bind him more tightly to Starkfield: "He no longer believed what Zeena had told him of the supposed seriousness of her state: he saw in her expedition to Bettsbridge only a plot hatched between herself and her Pierce relations to foist on him the cost of a servant; and for the moment wrath predominated" (120). When he disputes her hiring of someone he cannot afford to pay, however, she immediately reminds him of his responsibility for her condition. As she lost her health nursing his mother, he is required to provide all she requires for her comfort.

Zeena's charge is as false as her claims of serious illness, and Wharton subjects this figure to trenchant irony whenever she invokes the past and speaks of sacrifice. Ethan's cousin, Zeena Pierce originally came to the farm to help during the final months of his mother's life. Shrouded in silence for years after his widowed mother stopped speaking, Ethan heard music in the flow of Zeena's conversation and marveled at the effect of her deft touch on the farmhouse. Panicked at the thought of another silent winter, he proposed to Zeena as she was packing to leave following his mother's funeral. He married her with confidence in their plan to sell the family property and flee Starkfield for a larger, more vital town or city. Yet within a year, he knew that he would never take flight with Zeena: "She chose to look down on Starkfield, but she could not have lived in a place which looked down on her. Even Bettsbridge or Shadd's Falls would not have been sufficiently aware of her, and in the greater cities which attracted Ethan she would have suffered a complete loss of identity" (98). Too late, he came to see that her aptitude for nursing his mother had been the expression not of her vigor but of her affinity for the sickroom. Appropriating the role of invalid for herself soon after their marriage, Zeena constricted his future as well as her own.

Tracing the history of the Fromes' childless union, Wharton invites little sympathy for Zeena. Both Harmon Gow and Mrs. Hale assert that Ethan is the figure who has had " 'an awful mean time' " taking care of others, and the visiting engineer who narrates the story shares their view. Wharton's fiction is filled with unhappy marriages, and the Fromes' union is a particularly grim illustration of the lifetime of misery which can result from a wrong choice. Yet the transformation of lively Zeena Pierce into sullen, vindictive Zeena Frome also reflects the oppressive conditions of rural life in the Berkshires. The novel presents Zeena's retreat into silence after her marriage as a response to these conditions, attributing the change in her to "the inevitable effect of life on the farm" (98). The parallel which Wharton develops between Ethan's wife and his mother suggests the heavy toll of days spent in an isolated farmhouse removed from the rhythms of life in the village. Unable to understand or please Zeena, Ethan comes to fear that she may be falling prey to the "queerness" manifested by his mother and by other women in the region: "Zeena, who had at her fingers' ends the pathological chart of the whole region, had cited many cases of the kind while she was nursing his mother; and he himself knew of certain lonely farm-houses in the neighborhood where sudden tragedy had come of their presence" (99). In this broader context, her story becomes more than a coda to Ethan and Mattie's failed romance. Zeena's deepening discontent within a barren marriage cannot be assuaged, any more than her bright red pickle dish can be restored to wholeness.

When Ethan and Mattie fail in their suicide attempt, they change Zeena's life as irrevocably as their own. The immediate shifting of the two women's roles is one of the more ironic consequences of the "smash up." Zeena is forced to cede her identity as invalid to Mattie, for her own health appears robust next to the younger woman's catastrophic injuries. Mattie is incapable of working for the rest of her life, so Zeena is required to assume responsibility once again for the desolate farmhouse. More pointedly, the two women in Ethan Frome's life come to resemble each other closely. Living together in privation for more than twenty years, they become so indistinguishable in appearance and manner that Ethan surprises the narrator with his introductions on the night of the blizzard. The visitor's description of Mattie makes this connection between the women explicit: "Her hair was as gray as her companion's, her face as bloodless and shrivelled, but amber-tinted, with swarthy shadows sharpening the nose and hollowing the temples" (152). The similarities extend beyond angularity and coloring to temperament, for the woman "droning querulously" as the men enter the house is not Zeena but Mattie. Compared to a witch by the narrator,[14] Mattie complains in her chair with a virulence worthy of the younger Zeena. Tied to each other for the rest of their lives, Zeena and Mattie can derive no solace from their relationship. Trapped in a misshapen home with his wife and the woman he once preferred to her, Ethan can expect no peace until he takes his place in the family graveyard.

5

NARRATIVE ART

Reviewing her earlier progress as a writer, Wharton identifies *Ethan Frome* in her autobiography as the first project which allowed her to experience "the artisan's full control of his implements" (209). Although she recalls the period of writing which followed the success of *The House of Mirth* as one which gave her a "growing sense of mastery" over her fiction, she notes that the pleasure which she took in the creation of *Ethan Frome* was entirely new and invigorating (*Backward Glance* 293) In her various commentaries on the New England novel following its publication, Wharton expresses particular satisfaction with the work's narrative structure.[1] The novel's dense verbal texture is an even more impressive measure of her artistry, for *Ethan Frome* is shaped by interwoven patterns of imagery which extend and deepen characterization, setting and theme. Wharton relies on the continuing interplay of image and symbol to evoke a stricken world—a stark field of action—and the blasted figures dwelling in it. Using foreshadowing prominently, she dramatizes the pressure on these characters as they move ineluctably toward the novel's violent climax. Developing the action of *Ethan Frome* in a deliberately compressed form, Wharton derives much of her novel's power from a range of concentrated images and ironic contrasts.

WINTER, SILENCE AND DEATH

One of the most pervasive patterns of imagery within the novel associates Wharton's taciturn farmer with the season of winter. The snow and ice of the winter months in the Berkshires influence setting within *Ethan Frome*, and they also project the inner life of the protagonist. Although the novel spans two different periods in Ethan's life, all of its action unfolds in the fierce cold of this season. Darkly fascinated by the relentless quality of the winter weather which he experiences during his visit, the narrator uses richly metaphorical language to convey its effect on the village:

During the early part of my stay I had been struck by the contrast between the vitality of the climate and the deadness of the community. Day by day, after the December snows were over, a blazing blue sky poured down torrents of light and air on the white landscape, which gave them back in an intense glitter. One would have supposed that such an atmosphere must quicken the emotions as well as the blood; but it seemed to produce no change except that of retarding still more the sluggish pulse of Starkfield. When I had been there a little longer, and had seen this phase of crystal clearness followed by long stretches of sunless cold; when the storms of February had pitched their white tents about the devoted village and the wild cavalry of March winds had charged down to their support; I began to understand why Starkfield emerged from its six months' siege like a starved garrison capitulating without quarter. (65–66)

This poetic rendering of winter in New England establishes an important frame of reference for the novel. From the opening pages of the prologue, the narrator casts wintry Starkfield as a place of torpor ("the sluggish pulse"), lifelessness ("the deadness of the community") and privation ("a starved garrison"). Guided by Harmon Gow's pronouncement that Ethan has remained in this village "too many winters" (64), the narrator focuses closely on the conditions of the season in order to come to terms with the crippled figure trapped in it.

Recently arrived in Starkfield, this outsider is filled with curiosity the first time he sees Ethan struggling across the porch of the post office. What attracts his attention is not the nature of Ethan's limitations, however, but the expression on his weathered face. The narrator finds Ethan commanding even in his infirmity, and distinguished from all others in Starkfield by the appearance of "something bleak and unapproachable in his face" (63). Seeking to penetrate that expression, the narrator remains unsatisfied after his conversations with his driver Gow and his landlady Mrs. Hale: "no one gave me an explanation of the look in his face which, as I persisted in thinking, neither poverty nor physical suffering could have put there" (67). Relying unexpectedly on Ethan for transportation to the train each day, the narrator begins to draw his own conclusions about his new driver's character (and countenance). Rebuffed in his efforts at conversation, the narrator muses on Ethan's affinity with the icy countryside:

He never turned his face to mine, or answered, except in monosyllables, the questions I put, or such slight pleasantries as I ventured. He seemed a part of the mute melancholy landscape, an incarnation of its frozen woe, with all that was warm and sentient in him fast bound below the surface; but there was nothing unfriendly in his silence. I simply felt that he lived in a depth of moral isolation too remote for casual access, and I had the sense that his loneliness was not merely the result of his personal plight, tragic as I guessed that to be, but had in it, as Harmon Gow had hinted, the profound accumulated cold of too many Starkfield winters. (68–69)

Denied personal contact with Ethan, who withholds eye contact as well as conversation, the narrator perceives in him an extension of the frozen expanses surrounding them. Reflecting on the connection between the silent man and the desolate landscape, the narrator concentrates on the "depth of moral isolation" in which Ethan lives. He concludes that all that is vital ("warm and sentient") in Ethan's nature has been layered over with ice after so many winters in Starkfield.

Wharton elaborates upon this metaphor as the prologue draws to a close. References to winter dominate Ethan's infrequent attempts at conversation, suggesting how completely the season characterizes him. He uses a revealing metaphor when he responds to the engineer's words about the differences between balmy Florida and frigid Massachusetts: " 'Yes: I was down there once, and for a good while afterward I could call up the sight of it in winter. But now it's all snowed under' " (69). Ethan acknowledges hoarding these memories of his sojourn in Florida—where he was a fledging engineer, not a farmer—until they were "snowed under" and thus lost to him. His home is also "snowed under," even before the worsening of the storm which forces the narrator to take shelter there. Like the village of Starkfield, the Frome farm is portrayed in language of stagnation and want. The "exanimate" saw-mill is blanketed with snow, its neighboring sheds sagging under the accumulated weight of frost. The orchard and fields are buried under the same drifts of snow, though the former is distinguished by "starved apple-trees writhing over a hillside among outcroppings of slate that nuzzled up through the snow like animals pushing out their noses to breathe" (71). These images of starvation and suffocation frame Ethan's identification of his home, a forlorn farmhouse "huddled against the white immensities of land and sky" (71). Surveying the blankness of the snow swallowing up the Frome property, the narrator fancies that the house itself quakes from the cold wind.

As the story of Ethan Frome takes shape in the long flashback that follows, these frozen layers of snow and ice function as a tangible expression of his buried life within Starkfield. The metaphorical language of the prologue is sustained and refined throughout the narrative, reminding the reader how much of the protagonist's life is "snowed under." The opening chapters characterize Ethan as uncommunicative, even among New Englanders noted for their taciturnity. Chapter I presents him alone outside the church where Mattie Silver dances, increasingly lost in his private thoughts and fears about his marriage. Refreshed by her presence after the dance ends, he is nonetheless incapable of articulating his feelings in anything but a "growl of rapture" (85) when she dismisses Denis Eady in his cutter for her customary walk home with him. When Ethan soon frightens Mattie by alluding to her imminent departure from the farm, he cannot find the words which he needs to reassure her. Instead, he is described as "vainly [struggling] for expression" while she conveys her distress in a torrent of words (87).

Although this pattern remains a dominant one to the novel's climax, Wharton nonetheless characterizes Ethan as a man who longs to reveal his "secret soul" (79). Since his return from college in Worcester, he has been drawn into the deepening silence of first his mother and then his wife. Attracted to Mattie from her first months on the moribund farm, he nurtures the vague hope that she will restore his powers of expression, his experience of human connectedness. Anticipating his evening alone with her during Zeena's trip to Bettsbridge, he is freed to express his feelings in music (whistling, singing) as he considers the life which he once enjoyed outside the village limits:

There was in him a slumbering spark of sociability which the long Starkfield winters had not yet extinguished. By nature grave and inarticulate, he admired recklessness and gaiety in others and was warmed to the marrow by friendly human intercourse. At Worcester, though he had the name of keeping to himself and not being much of a hand at a good time, he had secretly gloried in being clapped on the back and hailed as "Old Ethe" or "Old Stiff"; and the cessation of such familiarities had deepened the chill of his return to Starkfield. (96–97)

This passage emphasizes the desire for friendly contact "slumbering" or buried in Ethan, even as it acknowledges the natural barrier of his passivity (see Chapter 4). The language of the passage reinforces the association of Starkfield with loneliness and cold, as well as the human cost of spending too many winters there. Shaped by this environment, Ethan finds that he must struggle to move out of self during his evening by the fire with Mattie. Subdued and even "paralysed" by reminders of the absent Zeena (104), he nearly forfeits his opportunity for private conversation with Mattie.

Against the background of wintry Shadow Pond, Ethan's inwardness is even more apparent. Near the end of his abortive romance with Mattie, he delays her return to the train at the Flats by bringing her to this isolated setting. An analogue for the protagonist's inner life, Shadow Pond is described by the narrator as "a shy secret spot, full of the same dumb melancholy that Ethan felt in his heart" (141). Ethan chooses this spot, site of a church picnic the previous year, for its association with summer and with rituals of courtship. Recalling his encounter with Mattie by the campfire on that summer day, he likens the pleasure they have shared to "inarticulate flashes, when they seemed to come suddenly upon happiness as if they had surprised a butterfly in the winter woods" (142).

This simile for their rare moments of happiness holds in tension the reality he knows ("inarticulate," "winter") with the markedly different one she knows ("flashes [of light]," "butterfly"). Longing to reveal the depth of his feelings to her in the limited time remaining to them, he finds himself unable to speak at Shadow Pond and so accompanies her back to the sled in unbroken silence.

The route from the lake at Shadow Pond to the tree on School House Hill proves to be short. The narrative of this journey relies on language of darkness and death as evening overtakes the Berkshires and Ethan and Mattie confront the inevitability of parting. Their drive to the Flats is presented as a falling motion: "They were silent again. They had reached the point where the road dipped to the hollow by Ethan's mill and as they descended the darkness descended with them, dropping down like a black veil from the heavy hemlock boughs" (144). The association of night with dark confusion ("black veil") and destructiveness ("hemlock") persists to the novel's denouement. All too aware of the anonymous future which she faces as part of the urban working class, Mattie is the one who proposes suicide on the icy hill. Goaded by her to consider the empty days and nights stretching out before him, Ethan contemplates the darkness of the spruces surrounding them and imagines that he and Mattie are already buried in their coffins underground. He assents to her proposal of suicide when he concludes that death will signify release from his turmoil, " 'After this I sha'n't feel anything' " (148).

The epilogue underscores the bitter irony of this sentiment, for Ethan's life twenty-four years after the "smash-up" is devoid of feeling. The middle-aged figure who survived the crash into the big elm tree is characterized as a man caught uncomfortably between life and death, as a man enduring a living death. His condition is established at the outset of the novel, when the visiting engineer disputes Gow's prediction that Ethan will reach the age of one hundred. " '*That* man touch a hundred? He looks as if he was dead and in hell now!' " (64). More dead than alive, Ethan is perceived by the narrator (and by most readers) as one who is indeed experiencing the tortures of the damned. The final conversation between the engineer and his landlady conveys powerfully the extent to which all three characters trapped in the Frome farmhouse have suffered since the failed suicide attempt. The family graveyard which Ethan passes every day inspires the novel's closing, as Mrs. Hale laments the fact that Mattie did not die from her terrible injuries. " 'And I say, if she'd ha' died, Ethan might ha' lived; and the way they are now, I don't see there's much difference between the Fromes up at the farm and the Fromes down in the graveyard; 'cept that down there they're all quiet, and the women have got to hold their tongues' " (156). With sympathy and regret, this choric figure conveys the lifelessness of Ethan Frome's existence. Plunged into winter too early, he awaits the release of death and the quiet of the graveyard.

THE LURE OF NATURE

A radiant presence in the novel, Mattie Silver appears to offer the younger Ethan Frome all that is missing from his life. With a name suggestive of luster as well as value, she is associated with language and imagery drawn largely from the world of nature. This pattern is not unique to Mattie, of course, for Ethan himself is described as an embodiment of Starkfield's frozen spaces. Yet Wharton assigns her qualities which contrast sharply with his defining traits. In the symbolic shorthand of the novel, Mattie is spring and Ethan is winter. She expresses herself with animation, in song as well as speech, and he moves in brooding silence. The romance which develops between them is organized around these opposing systems of imagery, as Wharton dramatizes the ways in which Mattie and Ethan have the potential to complement each other.

The world of nature gives this doomed romance its form as well as its texture. From the start of the novel, Wharton characterizes Ethan and Mattie as figures deeply sensitive to the natural beauty of the Berkshires. The exposition supplied in the first chapter advances this common trait as a basis for their relationship. Ethan began to draw closer to his wife's cousin when he made the unexpected discovery that she shared his delight in the sky and the land around them, for his enjoyment of nature had been entirely solitary and incommunicable to that point. His powers of observation sharpened by his interrupted studies in Worcester, he was accustomed to experiencing the beauty of the world as a "silent ache" (79) until Mattie joined him out of doors. Her enthusiasm for the beauty of a cloud formation or the color of a sunset then supplied an anodyne for his pain.

He did not even know whether any one else in the world felt as he did, or whether he was the sole victim of this mournful privilege. Then he learned that one other spirit had trembled with the same touch of wonder: that at this side, living under his roof and eating his bread, was a creature to whom he could say: "That's Orion down yonder; the big fellow to the right is Aldebaran, and the bunch of little ones—like bees swarming—they're the Pleiades..." or whom he could hold entranced before a ledge of granite thrusting up through the fern while he unrolled huge panorama of the ice age, and the long dim stretches of succeeding time. The fact that admiration for his learning mingled with Mattie's wonder at what he taught was not the least part of his pleasure. (79)

Expansive in the presence of another who sees the world as he does, Ethan uses a vocabulary inspired by nature (and fortified by college) to express his inmost self. Sharing the beauty of New England with Mattie provides Ethan with the language which he needs to "utter his secret soul" (79) and escape his isolation.

Nature also affords these two figures a sanctuary all their own. In the tradition of nineteenth-century Romanticism, *Ethan Frome* elevates the world of nature over the social order. Wharton establishes this dichotomy in the first two chapters of the novel and maintains it through the climax on School House Hill.[2] Nature is the site of freedom and spontaneity for Ethan and Mattie, the setting for those private walks which encourage them in their hopes of a future together. Chapter II conveys vividly the ease which they enjoy together outdoors, as they return from the village under a starlit sky. The conditions are inviting despite the time of year, the air itself "so dry and pure that it [gives] little sensation of cold" (75). In this rarefied atmosphere, Ethan and Mattie experience a closeness which is characterized as a "sweetness of...communion" (79). A Wordsworthian construct, the world of nature within the novel has the power to restore harmony to the lives of those who recognize its beauty.

All is dissonant in society, however, for the Frome farmhouse is a place of constriction and repression. Wharton emphasizes this tension at the close of Chapter II, when Ethan and Mattie's brief respite in nature ends with Zeena's dramatic opening of the kitchen door. The moment is deliberately delayed, long enough that Ethan toys with the thought that his wife has somehow died in his absence. Finding the key missing from its customary place under the mat, Ethan and Mattie are positioned awkwardly outside the door when it opens suddenly. The appearance of Zeena on the threshold is particularly jarring to Ethan:

Against the dark background of the kitchen she stood up tall and angular, one hand drawing a quilted counterpane to her flat breast, while the other held a lamp. The light, on a level with her chin, drew out of that darkness her puckered throat and the projecting wrist of the hand that clutches the quilt, and deepened fantastically the hollows and prominences of her high-boned face under its ring of crimping pins. To Ethan, still in the rosy haze of his hour with Mattie, the sight came with the intense precision of the last dream before waking. He felt as if he had never before known what his wife looked like. (89–90)

The language of the passage enforces the continuing division between inside and outside, portraying Zeena as a grim usher or gatekeeper. Her appearance in the harsh lamplight is defined by angles and shadows, her identification with the domestic realm secured by the quilt she clutches and the curling pins she sports. As Ethan and Mattie wordlessly cross the threshold and enter the kitchen, they forsake the purity of the night air for the "deadly chill of a vault" (90).

The Romantic tension between nature and civilization generated in this opening sequence influences much of the action that follows. The house to which Ethan and Mattie return after the church dance is a poor alternative to the starry night, and the change in their demeanor is pronounced. Climbing the hill to the house, they enjoy the sensation of "floating on a summer stream" (88). Crossing the threshold, they enter a cramped space regulated by Zeena and thus feel constrained immediately. The mortal chill of the kitchen drives all three figures upstairs (though Ethan makes a feint at remaining below and avoiding the bedroom he shares with his wife). The kitchen is no more inviting in daylight the next morning, when Ethan returns reluctantly from the fields for breakfast. His discovery that Zeena is leaving on an overnight trip encourages him to hope that Mattie will restore the kitchen to its former warmth and cheer. Leaving for his day's work, he fancies that the room is already sunnier and brighter with Mattie installed in Zeena's place. Yet he finds the room itself inhibiting when he is alone with Mattie by the fire that night. "He knew that most young men made nothing at all of giving a pretty girl a kiss, and he remembered that the night before, when he had put his arm about Mattie, she had not resisted. But that had been out-of-doors, under the open irresponsible night. Now, in the warm lamplit room, with all its ancient implications of conformity and order, she seemed infinitely farther away and more unapproachable" (109). For Ethan, this room somehow embodies those conventions and mores of nineteenth-century New England life which separate him from Mattie.

The lure of "irresponsible nature" is so strong that the novel's climax takes place under the evening sky. Emphasizing the circularity of Ethan's movements in the novel, Wharton sets the beginning and ending scenes (Chapters I and IX) under the same dark trees on School House Hill. Joseph X. Brennan points to the symbolic effect of these black spruces, arguing that they are vital to the ongoing contrast between nature and society: "Of the many natural objects and locations which constitute the pattern of outdoor imagery, the two black Norway spruces are surely the most important, since they provide the setting for the lovers' uttermost passion and fatal final resolve" (350). Ethan and Mattie begin their brief romance under the shelter of these trees in Chapter II, when he triumphantly claims her for their two-mile walk to the farmhouse. Ned Hale and Ruth Varnum take the place of Ethan and Mattie the next afternoon, kissing in the privacy afforded by the spruces (Chapter IV). Discovering the engaged couple, Ethan is characteristically divided in his response. He takes pleasure in the sight of their embrace, but then feels all the more keenly the furtiveness of his relations with Mattie. The final romantic liaison under the dark trees emphasizes the difference between the two couples, for it is in this spot that Mattie makes her desperate bid for suicide. In a Romantic affirmation of nature's superiority, Mattie persuades Ethan to choose the open space stretching below them over the barren farmhouse waiting for him.

SPRING, MUSIC AND VITALITY

To the climactic moment on top of School House Hill, Mattie Silver represents warmth and the promise of renewal for Ethan Frome. Frozen in place too long, he looks to her for release from the cold and silence of winter. Admiring her initially for her responsiveness to natural beauty, he soon identifies her with the rhythms of springtime. The tentative beginnings of their relationship are supplied in Chapter I, as Ethan strides through the snow to fetch her home from the church dance. He finds himself remembering her arrival by train a year earlier, a frail young woman who seemed incapable of the housework Zeena expected. Even as Mattie recovered from her punishing stint behind a shop counter, she brought new life to the farmhouse. Specifically, her presence in his home affected Ethan "like the lighting of a fire on a cold hearth" (78). The striking image conflates light and heat, two qualities essential to Mattie's role in the novel.

The narrative of the two figures' walk home (Chapter II) develops this pattern of imagery further. Fearful that Mattie will accept Denis Eady's offer of a ride in his cutter, Ethan remains hidden from view as the villagers disperse after the dance. Happy when Ethan reveals himself to her, Mattie is soon astonished to learn that he was present during her conversation with Denis. Her good-natured questions about Ethan's eavesdropping provoke his laughter—and a melting of the tension deep within him. "Her wonder and his laughter ran together like spring rills in a thaw" (85). The simile inaugurates a pattern which extends and deepens Mattie's characterization. In her company, Ethan feels the warmth of spring and dares to dream of renewal. In language which becomes insistent in Chapter II, the novel's introduction of Ethan with Mattie, she warms his lifeblood and dispels the mortal chill he has known.

He forgot what else he had meant to say and pressed her against him so closely that he seemed to feel her warmth in his veins.... But now all desire for change had vanished, and the sight of the little enclosure [the family graveyard] gave him a warm sense of continuance and stability.... Half-way up the slope Mattie stumbled against some unseen obstruction and clutched his sleeve to steady herself. The wave of warmth that went through him was like the prolongation of his vision. For the first time he stole his arm about her, and she did not resist. They walked on as if they were floating on a summer stream. (88)

Joyful and easy in the dark, Ethan is emboldened to reach out to Mattie and hold her. His growing confidence is conveyed by an attendant progression in the image pattern, from spring rills to summer streams.

Wharton aligns Mattie with these seasons of warmth and growth throughout the novel, using metaphors which accumulate power by the closing chapter. When Ethan attempts to keep Mattie close after she has been banished, for example, he is distracted by the scent of her hair. Hoping to comfort her at the start of Chapter IX, he kisses her hair and registers that it is "soft yet springy, like certain mosses on warm slopes, and [has] the faint woody fragrance of fresh sawdust in the sun" (138). The sensual detail is inviting, the invocation of sun and heat alluring. Ethan feels the same stirrings of desire after Mattie begs him to end their lives on School House Hill. He moves quickly from resistance to acquiescence when he strokes her hair and finds himself released from the tyranny of winter: "Her pleadings still came to him between short sobs, but he no longer heard what she was saying. Her hat had slipped back and he was stroking her hair. He wanted to get the feeling of it into his hand, so that it would sleep there like a seed in winter. Once he found her mouth again, and they seemed to be by the pond together in the burning August sun" (148). Ethan's desire to preserve the memory of Mattie's hair is captured in language which completes a complex pattern of imagery within the novel. A farmer contemplating death, Ethan holds fast to Mattie and thinks of the seed buried in the ground which will spring to life again.[3]

A different pattern of imagery associated with Mattie is decidedly ethereal. Again and again in the novel, her gestures (and even her thoughts) are compared to the movements of a bird. The effect of the pattern is to emphasize her delicacy and sheer attractiveness to Ethan, who imputes to her a lightness of spirit which he lacks. Recalling her return to health on the farm, he thinks of how she thrived in the "pure air, and long summer hours" of the open countryside (93). Seeking only to spend time in her presence, he occasionally finds that he cannot keep pace with her thoughts and her changing moods: "The motions of her mind were as incalculable as the flit of a bird in the branches" (86). Yet Ethan remains tantalized to the novel's climax, yearning for her freedom and grace. Merely watching her sew gives him pleasure during their evening alone in the farmhouse; he sits in "fascinated contemplation" as her hands move back and forth across the cloth "just as he had seen a pair of birds make short perpendicular flights over a nest they were building" (110). The comparison is deftly complex, revealing Ethan's desire to build a home ("nest") with this lovely young woman who resembles a bird in flight.

Another source of Ethan's wordless fascination for Mattie is her openness, her ready delight in conversation. Her laughter animates her early meetings with Ethan, who hears an echo of her merriment in the song of a bird. As he walks to town in Chapter VIII, intent on finding a way to keep her with him, he is arrested by the resemblance: "Once, in the stillness, the call of a bird in a mountain ash was so like her laughter that his heart tightened and then grew large" (134–35). Feeling keenly the limitations of a silent wife whom he perceives as "bitter" and "querulous" (129), he depends increasingly on his relationship with her younger, livelier cousin. From the time Ethan meets Mattie at the train, she is defined by her ability to express herself in ways which he cannot muster. "He had taken to the girl from the first day, when he had driven over to the Flats to meet her, and she had smiled and waved to him from the train, crying out 'You must be Ethan!' as she jumped down with her bundles" (78). She speaks throughout the novel with a volubility he envies, for much of his experience remains incommunicable. In her presence, however, he is roused to attempt the sort of conversation which he enjoyed as a student in Worcester.

An even stronger measure of Mattie's élan is her association with the novel's snatches of music. Her first appearance in *Ethan Frome* is framed by music and dance, when Ethan hovers in the shadows outside the village church waiting to walk her home (Chapter I). Peering in a window, he watches as the crowded room is transformed by the stirrings of one final set, an energetic Virginia reel. Dismayed, Ethan registers Mattie's joy as she responds to the rhythms of the music and takes her place by Denis Eady. She is one with the lively dance, moving up and down the line in a blur of "laughing panting lips, the cloud of dark hair about her forehead, and the dark eyes which seemed the only fixed points in a maze of flying lines" (77). Although Ethan will not join in the harmony of this dance, he is soon inspired by her example of song (and by news of Zeena's imminent departure for Bettsbridge). Hearing Mattie hum music from the dance as she works at the kitchen sink the next morning, he finds himself whistling and even singing out loud on his way into town (Chapter IV). Anticipating an evening alone with her, he adopts her lilting idiom to express his pleasure.

Mattie's importance to Ethan is accented by color as well as by music, for she is presented as a character offering him the passion missing from his marriage to Zeena. Wharton emphasizes the vitality of Mattie throughout the novel, most often through the use of color imagery. Shades of red and scarlet distinguish Mattie from all others in the snow-covered world of Starkfield, granting her a vibrancy which Ethan cannot resist. When he peers into the church basement window in Chapter I, he has no difficulty identifying Mattie from a distance. She is the woman at the center of the gathering who is wearing a bright scarf, "a cherry-coloured 'fascinator'" (77). Mattie's capacity to fascinate Ethan is dramatized on the two-mile walk that follows the dance, leaving him to face his gaunt wife in a "rosy haze" (89). The color red is even more prominent in an ironic reversal of this encounter between Ethan and Zeena, when he returns home the next evening to find Mattie waiting for him on the same threshold. The contrast between the two women in the Frome household is defined by the vivid color which Mattie has chosen to mark the occasion:

She wore her usual dress of darkish stuff, and there was no bow at her neck; but through her hair she had run a streak of crimson ribbon. This tribute to the unusual transformed and glorified her. She seemed to Ethan taller, fuller, more womanly in shape and motion. She stood aside, smiling silently, while he entered, and then moved away from him with something soft and flowing in her gait. (103)

Wearing a band of bright red in her dark hair, Mattie assumes new proportions in the novel. She appears grander and more sensual to Ethan, and their evening together is immediately charged with additional significance.

Wharton steadily identifies Mattie with red, the color of passion in literary tradition. This imagery serves theme as well as characterization, and it organizes the tentative beginnings of Ethan's romance with Mattie. He sees the red geraniums which she is nursing through the New England winter and thinks of the small garden which he created for her the previous summer. He remembers how she looked "pretty as a picture" at the Shadow Pond church picnic which began their courtship, "bright as a blackberry bush under her spreading [pink] hat" (142). He meets her in her empty room on the day of her departure and recalls the red and white quilt which he once saw on her bed. These vivid splashes of color, extending from Mattie's choice of flower to the covering on her bed, represent the vitality which separates her firmly from Zeena.

This principle of division is made explicit in the novel's most prominent use of the color red, the pickle dish which Mattie selects for her dinner with Ethan. She chooses this "gay red glass" (103) in hopes of making their weekday meal more festive, but the dish takes on much greater significance after it is broken. Kenneth Bernard points to the positioning of this episode at the novel's center, arguing the "sexual symbolism" of the pickle dish which Zeena has refused to use through all the years of her childless marriage. A wedding gift from Zeena's Aunt Philura Maple, the red dish which Mattie fills with Ethan's favorite pickles symbolizes fertility as well as passion. Peter L. Hays emphasizes the irony of this association between the dish and the wedding, suggesting that Wharton intends the sourness of pickles to convey the character of the Frome marriage (Item #15).

The breaking of the glass at the end of Chapter IV thus has far-reaching consequences, for Zeena cares for this dish above all other possessions. When she finds the broken shards of glass hidden from view in the kitchen cupboard, she treats them as proof that her place in the household has been usurped by Mattie. For Zeena, Mattie's use of the cherished red dish is an act of unforgivable betrayal (Bernard 183). The wronged wife, she attacks Mattie with unprecedented emotion:

"You're a bad girl, Mattie Silver, and I always known it. It's the way your father begun, and I was warned of it when I took you, and I tried to keep my things where you couldn't get at em—and now you've took from me the one I cared for most of all—" She broke off in a short spasm of sobs that passed and left her more than ever like a shape of stone.

"If I'd 'a' listened to folks, you'd 'a' gone before now, and this wouldn't 'a' happened," she said; and gathering up the bits of broken glass she went out of the room as if she carried a dead body . . . " (128)

The language of this fierce denunciation reveals how deeply Zeena resents Mattie's more passionate nature. Exposing the torpor of Zeena in potent imagery of stasis ("shape of stone") and death ("dead body"), Wharton also intimates the fate of Mattie's vitality in the depleted world of the novel. The "bad girl" defined by the color red in her youth will become the sallow-faced invalid waiting for the release of death.

THE BLACK LANDSCAPE

The subtle interplay of shadows and light in this world provides another measure of Wharton's artistic control. Alternating images of light and dark are pervasive throughout the novel, deepening characterization and advancing theme. A compressed narrative of Ethan Frome's inner life, the novel unfolds against the dark background of the Berkshires in winter. The defeated figure whom we meet in the prologue spends his days in a monochromatic world of white snow and black shadow. His story begins to take shape on a night of impenetrable darkness, when he and the narrator are plunged into the "smothering medium" of a sudden blizzard (73). Forced to take shelter at the farm, the narrator enters the dark house with his host and sees enough in the harsh light of the kitchen to spark his "vision" of a younger Ethan and Mattie (74). In the narrative that follows, Mattie becomes the vibrant young woman with the power to dispel the darkness of Ethan's life. Her arrival in Starkfield one year earlier signified the promise of warmth and light for him, and he recalls in the first chapter how quickly she transformed his home. From the start, he experienced her presence in the farmhouse as "the lighting of a fire on a cold hearth" (78). The striking image functions much like her surname "Silver,"[4] establishing her as a center of light within the novel.

The first two chapters are structured by the contrast between the darkness Ethan knows and the light Mattie radiates. On his way to meet her at the opening of the novel, he moves through a moonless night past drifts of snow stained gray and black. The two black spruce trees by the Varnum house mark his entrance to the quiet village, where the only light emanates from the church with the white steeple: "The hush of midnight lay on the village, and all its waking life was gathered behind the church windows, from which strains of dance-music flowed with the broad bands of yellow light" (76). Ethan clings to the darkness outside, while Mattie relishes the glowing life inside the church. The room in which she dances is an oasis of light and heat, featuring gas jets, gleaming white walls and ovens which seem to be fuelled by "volcanic fires" (76). Looking on from the shadows, Ethan chafes at the way Mattie's face lights with pleasure at the end of a reel: "The face she lifted to her dancers was the same which, when she saw him, always looked like a window that caught the sunset" (79). Ethan's lovely tribute to Mattie is not without ambiguity. Fearful of her joy in the company of others, he honors her capacity for joy by associating her with light that dims and fades at day's end.

Increasingly diffident as the dance ends, Ethan tests Mattie by hiding in the dark and spying on her exchange with Denis Eady. Wharton uses the metaphor of a "black void" to convey the depth of Ethan's anxiety while he waits. Ethan feels himself dangling over a chasm until Mattie rebuffs her suitor and sets out alone for the farm: "Frome's heart, which had swung out over a black void, trembled back to safety" (84). Saved from the void—for a time—Ethan presents himself to a startled Mattie as she passes underneath the black Varnum spruces. Their furtive romance begins in this dark space, as he brandishes his knowledge of Denis' overtures and then takes her arm proprietarily. The same dark shade that will enshroud them in Chapter IX envelops them at this moment: "They stood together in the gloom of the spruces, an empty world glimmering about them wide and grey under the stars. . . . It was so dark under the spruces that he could barely see the shape of her head beside his shoulder. He longed to stoop his cheek and rub it against her scarf. He would have liked to stand there with her all night in the blackness" (85). Ethan's tender view of this "blackness" is undermined by the tone of the passage. The darkness of the trees prevails so completely that he cannot see the woman he desires. The shelter of the trees is actually "gloom," the starlit world surrounding the couple "empty."

Ethan remains in this figurative darkness for much of the novel, looking to Mattie to supply the deficiencies of his life. Walking by her side through the winter night, he sheds the vague fears which overtook him in the village and is lulled into complacency about their future together. Watching her working alone in the kitchen the next morning, he imagines that she has already restored the room to its former brightness and cheer. He sees her illuminated by sunbeams as she moves about the room, and he lingers in the doorway remembering how "'spruce' and shining" the kitchen once was (96). He marvels at the palpable difference Zeena's absence makes, a difference expressed in light images throughout Chapters IV and V. When he returns to the kitchen at day's end, he is heartened by the welcome which Mattie has prepared for him: "She set the lamp on the table, and he saw that it was carefully laid for supper, with fresh dough-nuts, stewed blueberries and his favourite pickles in a dish of gay red glass. A bright fire glowed in the stove and the cat lay stretched before it, watching the table with a drowsy eye" (103). Fearful that she has been entertaining Denis Eady in the empty farmhouse, however, he cannot trust the scene before him until he confirms that Jotham Powell has been her only visitor. The jealousy tormenting Ethan is imaged as "blackness," the relief from jealousy as light flooding his brain (104). This metaphor of beneficent light is extended through Chapter V, as Mattie sews by the lamp and he basks in their newfound intimacy. When she lights their way up the stairs at night's end, the candle which she carries before her "[makes] her dark hair look like a drift of mist on the moon" (111).

Zeena's return from Bettsbridge the next afternoon is etched in shades of gray and black, with neither moon nor mist softening her confrontation with her husband. Approaching the threshold of their bedroom, he finds her seated alone in the gathering shadows: "The room was almost dark, but in the obscurity her saw her sitting by the window, bolt upright, and knew by the rigidity of the outline projected against the pane that she had not taken off her traveling dress" (118). Viewing his wife from the doorway, Ethan sees only darkness and inflexibility in Zeena's form. He ventures a laconic comment about her journey, but he does not actually enter the "dim room" until she tells him that she is more seriously ill than he realizes. And his concern over her newly diagnosed "complications" founders quickly when she tells him of the steps she has taken to secure proper help in the farmhouse.

The bitter argument that follows, the first open conflict of Ethan and Zeena's marriage, takes place at twilight as the room falls into deeper shadow. Trading rancorous words about their life together, the two seem to embody the darkness of their bedroom: "Through the obscurity which hid their faces their thoughts seemed to dart at each other like serpents shooting venom. Ethan was seized with horror of the scene and shame at his own share in it. It was as senseless and savage as a physical fight between two enemies in the darkness" (120). Bereft of light, Ethan and Zeena strike out blindly at each other with a viciousness that appalls him. The language of the passage recalls the famous closing image of Matthew Arnold's 1851 poem, "Dover Beach."

> And we are here as on a darkling plain
> Swept with confused alarms of struggle and flight,
> Where ignorant armies clash by night. (ll. 35–37)

The "darkling plain" of Arnold's dramatic monologue might be the room in which Ethan stands, contending with a woman who has come to represent all that he finds oppressive. In an effort to stem the flow of bitter words, Ethan lights the room's only candle. He regains control over himself as he strikes the match, but the flickering light does little to combat the darkness of the setting. The triumph of the gathering shadows is complete when Zeena tells Ethan that she is sending Mattie away.

The darkness dominating this encounter persists to the novel's closing. When Ethan returns to the kitchen, he has begun moving through a "black landscape" which even Mattie cannot light. Unaware of her fate—and happily anticipating another meal alone with Ethan—she takes her seat and is described as "[shining] across the table" at him (124). Consumed by his own misery, he makes no effort to prepare her for the news of her leave taking, but delivers it jaggedly while kissing her. Her unsteady response to his exclamation inspires one of the final light images of the narrative: "The words went on sounding between them as though a torch of warning flew from hand to hand through a black landscape" (124). This image of a single warning light moving by relay across a dark terrain conveys the sense of urgency in the two figures, and thus the changing tone of the work as a whole. The lighted torch cannot overcome the blackness, much as Ethan and Mattie cannot overcome the circumstances arrayed against them. Anticipating the loss of her, he sees himself trapped in darkness until he dies: "There was no way out—none. He was a prisoner for life, and now his one ray of light was to be extinguished" (131).

Only one day intervenes between this eventful night and the next atop School House Hill, and its pale light offers fleeting comfort to the pair. Rising in the morning to find Mattie about her chores in the kitchen, Ethan feels an immediate release from the turmoil of his long night. Telling himself that she will not be separated from him after all, he chooses to view the "return of daylight" as a sign that Zeena will recant her threat (133). Buoyed by this hope, he sets out for the barn and is further reassured by the customary sight of his hired hand climbing the hill. The confused state of Ethan's thoughts is suggested by the "morning mist" (133) cloaking Jotham Powell, however, for change is imminent on the farm despite the play of light. Zeena's course has not been altered by the break of day; Ethan soon learns that she has already arranged for another neighbor to collect Mattie's trunk for the 5:00 train. He escapes the farm for the village, but cannot bring himself to betray the confidence of the Hales in order to secure a more lasting escape from Starkfield. He does not fare much better when he brings Mattie to Shadow Pond at day's end, for their visit takes place within a darkening stand of trees dwarfed by "the long conical shadow which gave the lake its name" (141). Wharton emphasizes the desolation of the scene at sunset as the two make their way to Starkfield: "The clumps of trees in the snow seemed to draw together in ruffled lumps, like birds with their heads under their wings; and the sky, as it paled, rose higher, leaving the earth more alone" (143). Drawn from the familiar world of nature, these distorted images of snow, birds and sky express the defeat of Ethan's hopes and dreams.

The remaining action of the novel unfolds in a deepening darkness which mirrors the couple's desperation. As Ethan and Mattie make their way to Starkfield, down the hill past the Frome saw mill, the darkness is described as descending with them, "dropping down like a black veil from the heavy hemlock boughs" (144). Caught in this blackness, they perceive their separation from the rhythms of life in the village below them. The pointed contrast is organized by light/dark imagery: "A cutter, mounting the road from the village, passed them by in a joyous flutter of bells, and they straightened themselves and looked ahead with rigid faces. Along the main street lights had begun to shine from the house-fronts and stray figures were turning in here and there at the gates" (145). Lacking either light or sanctuary, Ethan and Mattie find their way to the black Varnum spruces and attempt the bittersweet pleasure of coasting down the hill together one last time. Before they begin their sled ride, however, Mattie comments dubiously that it is "dreadfully dark," and Ethan privately acknowledges the hour as the most "confusing" of the evening (146). Their second journey down the hill, inspired by Mattie's desire for death, fulfills the novel's sustained pattern of light/dark imagery by drawing out the implications of the shadows in Ethan's life. Embracing Mattie under the dark trees, he imagines that the darkness signifies death: "The spruces swathed them in blackness and silence. They might have been in their coffins underground" (148). These conditions of blackness and silence endure through the novel's climax, as Ethan seeks to claim his death by steering the sled into the looming elm tree. Denied the death he sought, he awakens to find the blackness and silence replaced by the light of a single star and the unfamiliar sounds of a small animal crying in pain. In the details of this bleak denouement, Wharton conveys the shadowy quality of the life remaining to Ethan Frome.

THE INEXORABLE FACTS

Wharton marshals nuances of tone expertly as she prepares the violent end of *Ethan Frome*. In his early study of her fiction, Blake Nevius praises her accomplishment, calling attention to the "technical resourcefulness brought into play by the peculiar difficulties of telling Ethan's story" (128). Analyzing the seamless connection between setting and theme throughout the novel, Nevius suggests that the familiar landscape of the Berkshires inspired "symbol-making activity" unique in Wharton's career (129). The unyielding blankness of the winter landscape exerts pressures in other ways, and even the visiting engineer feels its heft. He muses on the enervating effect of so much ice and snow, perceiving an entire community transformed by the long winter. The same frozen expanses frame Ethan's acknowledgment of the "inexorable facts" of his captivity (131), the futility of his efforts to escape either his unhappy marriage or his hardscrabble farm. Wharton makes prominent use of ironic foreshadowing as she shapes this recognition, thus achieving a steadily darkening tone within the work as a whole.

The early chapter introducing Ethan and Mattie as a couple reveals the subtlety of Wharton's irony. Alone in the bracing night air, the two figures linger on the hill by the church before setting out for the farm (and Zeena). Mattie speaks almost wistfully of the moonlit coasting which took place there earlier in the evening, and Ethan invites her to return with him the following night to join the company. She accepts with alacrity, though not without noting the danger associated with sledding. Two friends of hers recently escaped (narrowly) a fatal crash at the foot of the hill, involving a tree described throughout the novel as "the big elm": " 'Ned Hale and Ruth

Varnum came just as *near* running into the big elm at the bottom. We were all sure they were killed.' Her shiver ran down his arm. 'Wouldn't it have been too awful? They're so happy!' " (86). Standing close enough to Mattie to feel her tremor as his own, Ethan responds by boasting about the reliability of his steering. He lingers over her exclamation, " 'They're so happy!,' " wanting to believe that the words describe Mattie and him rather than her friends. Ethan pursues this identification with Ned and Ruth for the rest of the novel, seeing their courtship as a tangible expression of his desire for a life with Mattie. Goaded by her description of the engaged couple, Ethan seeks her assurance that she will not be afraid to coast down the hill with him when the time comes.

Wharton undermines her protagonist further with another pointed reminder of death. Near the end of Chapter II, Ethan passes the Frome graveyard, dotted with tombstones long familiar to him. Accustomed to seeing these graves as mocking reminders of ancestors who never broke free of the farm, he finds himself viewing them differently with Mattie by his side. Expansive in the knowledge that she has no intention of leaving Starkfield, he now regards the markers as promises of continuity and stasis. All he seeks from life, he thinks, is the chance to remain on the farm with Mattie until he dies. " 'I guess we'll never let you go, Matt,' he whispered, as though even the dead, lovers once, must conspire with him to keep her; and brushing by the graves, he thought: 'We'll always go on living here together, and some day she'll lie there beside me' " (88). Wharton emphasizes the strength of this sentiment in her protagonist, referring to it in the paragraph that follows as "vision" and as "dream[s]" (88). The sentiment is neither vision nor dream, of course, but ironic foreshadowing of the bitter aftermath of his suicide attempt. David Eggenschwiler connects this early reverie of Ethan's to Mrs. Hale's closing words on the similarities between the Fromes in the graveyard and the Fromes in the farmhouse, suggesting that her comments reveal "his wishes [in Chapter II] symbolically fulfilled and telescoped" (245). Ethan's grim fate is to realize his dream—and to spend the rest of his life on the farm with both Mattie and Zeena, waiting for the release of death and the quiet of the graveyard.

As the novel continues, Wharton generates growing tension through her characters' repeated references to the big elm on School House Hill. From his first conversation about coasting with Mattie, Ethan nurtures the hope of an adventure with her in the romantic moonlight. His plan to bring her back to town the evening after the church dance changes when Zeena unexpectedly leaves them alone together in the farmhouse. Enjoying the freedom of private conversation with Mattie by the fire, he has no interest in coasting on this dark night. He continues to savor the prospect of taking her down the hill, however, and promises to do so the following evening. Shy and awkward even with Mattie, Ethan derives a sense of power from his physical superiority and encourages her to believe that only he can steer her safely over the difficult terrain. To fortify his position, he embellishes the danger of coasting past the big elm.

"Would you be scared to go down the Corbury road with me on a night like this?" he asked.
    Her cheeks burned redder. "I ain't any more scared than you are!"
    "Well, I'd be scared, then; I wouldn't do it. That's an ugly corner down by the big elm. If a fellow didn't keep his eyes open he'd go plumb into it." He luxuriated in the sense of protection and authority which his words conveyed. To prolong and intensify the feeling he added: "I guess we're well enough here." (108)

This dialogue does much more than strengthen the sense of peril associated with the act of sledding on School House Hill. Laden with Whartonian irony, the exchange exposes Ethan's weakness and his capacity for self-deception. At the climax, he will be more "scared" than Mattie to go down the hill again. He will also aim for the "ugly corner down by the big elm"—and miss it.
    This pivotal failure of Ethan's reveals the complexity of Wharton's narrative art. He agrees to coast into the treacherous landmark and end his life and Mattie's, rather than return to the house he shares with his older, dyspeptic wife. Cowed by Zeena for much of the novel, he never musters the strength to overturn her decisions or defy her openly. His response is instead inaction or retreat, a pattern inaugurated when he follows her meekly to bed at the end of Chapter II. When he nears the table eagerly in Chapter IV, to enjoy his meal alone with Mattie, he is unmanned by the mere mention of his absent wife's name and momentarily "paralysed" (104). When he directs Mattie to take Zeena's rocking chair after supper, he experiences a horrifying vision: "It was almost as if the other face, the face of the superseded woman, had obliterated that of the intruder" (107). Stunned by this vision of Zeena's face on Mattie's body, Ethan uses the language of destruction ("obliterated") to describe his wife's imagined effect on the woman he loves. When Mattie quickly abdicates the seat, a shaken Ethan makes no attempt to dissuade her. Zeena's influence is even more potent as Ethan attempts suicide two nights later, and her face interposes itself between the tree and him. "The big tree loomed bigger and closer, and as they bore down on it he thought: 'It's waiting for us: it seems to know.' But suddenly his wife's face, with twisted monstrous lineaments, thrust itself between him and his goal, and he made an instinctive movement to brush it aside" (150). Seeking death in nature, Ethan personifies the tree as a sentient being waiting patiently for Mattie and him. Aiming for the elm, he faces instead a distorted representation of Zeena, swelled to "monstrous" size in his imagination and wielding the power to determine once again his course of action.

When Ethan fails to right the course of the rushing sled, he is consigned to a living death with this woman (and her rival). The irony is complete when he regains consciousness and imagines that he is pinned under a boulder or a "monstrous load" (151). Wharton's repetition of the adjective "monstrous" to describe both Ethan's wife and his self-inflicted injury secures the connection between the two desperate choices which define his life within the novel. To convey Mattie's different fate after the crash, Wharton inverts some of the richer metaphorical language associated with this figure. The lovely young woman who reminds Ethan of a bird again and again during her year at the farmhouse is initially unrecognizable to him at the foot of the elm tree. As a result of the accident, bird-like Mattie is reduced to a whimpering field mouse, a creature earthbound and common. When the narrator meets her years later, on the night of the blizzard, she no longer bears any resemblance to the character who once warmed and brightened Ethan's life "like the lighting of a fire on a cold hearth." Her petulant voice dominates the brief encounter in the kitchen, and her subject is the cold hearth. Apologizing to his guest for the temperature of the room, Ethan assumes that the fire has died. Mattie's complaint is pointed and swift, " 'It's on'y just been made up this very minute. Zeena fell asleep and slep' ever so long, and I thought I'd be frozen stiff before I could wake her up and get her to 'tend to it' " (152–53). "Frozen stiff" himself, Ethan makes no effort to placate Mattie as Zeena enters the room with the remains of a cold pie. With his final terse words of the novel, he presents to the narrator the unhappy women who share the misshapen farmhouse with him.

6

RECEPTION

The most famous work of Edith Wharton's long career, *Ethan Frome* did not initially attract the wide readership which *The House of Mirth* enjoyed in 1905. The short novel was published serially in *Scribner's Magazine* from August through October 1911 for the fee of $2,500. It appeared in book form at the end of September 1911 simultaneously in New York (Charles Scribner's Sons) and London (Macmillan). (*Ethan Frome* was also published several months later in France, in the February 1912 issue of *Revue des deux mondes*, under the title *Sous la neige* or *Under the Snow*.) Wharton received an advance of $2,000 for the novel from Scribner's, and her correspondence with her publisher following its American release expresses vividly her dissatisfaction with the pace of the book's sales and the advertising efforts on its behalf. In the first six weeks following publication of the book, forty-two hundred copies were sold. Hoping for a second edition, Wharton attempted to challenge these sales figures at the end of November, assuring her publisher that a friend "who sailed about November 1st" learned in Brentano's bookstore that *Ethan Frome* was the most sought after novel of the season (*Letters* 263). This anecdote had no effect on Scribner's sales figures, though Wharton received an additional advance of $1,000 against royalties.[1] The number of copies sold rose to nearly seven thousand by the end of February 1912 when Scribner's assured her that the work was "still in active demand" (Lewis 311). Yet Wharton would remain disappointed in the popular response to her Berkshire tale for the next two decades, until the work attracted growing numbers of readers in the closing years of her life.

REVIEWS

The critical response to *Ethan Frome* was much more satisfying for Wharton than the popular one. Although early sales of the novel lagged behind her expectations, the encouragement which she received from friends and reviewers was swift and emphatic. A favorite guest at her home in Lenox, Henry James enjoyed accompanying her on long drives through the towns and villages which had inspired the creation of Starkfield. He wrote to Wharton from England soon after the novel's publication, expressing his pleasure in the finished work: "I exceedingly admire, sachez Madame, *Ethan Frome*. A beautiful art & tone & truth—a beautiful artful *kept-down-ness,* & yet effective cumulation. It's a 'gem'—& excites great admiration here…" (*James and Wharton Letters* 195).[2] Theodore Roosevelt wrote to convey his admiration, noting in a letter that his wife turned eagerly to *Ethan Frome* at the start of her recovery from a serious accident. A regular correspondent since the earlier years of his presidency—and an avid fellow reader—Roosevelt described the novel to Wharton as "one of the most powerful things you have done" (*Letters of Roosevelt* 436). The praise which Francis P. Kinnicutt lavished on the novel was more poignant, if no less enthusiastic. Her troubled husband's attending physician, Kinnicutt knew the strain under which Wharton labored as she wrote *Ethan Frome* during the winter of 1910–1911. Calling the work "a classic that will be read and re-read with pleasure and instruction," he emphasizes in a letter dated December 1, 1911, his amazement at what Wharton was able to achieve in the midst of such "pressing anxieties" (qtd. in Lewis 310).

With few exceptions, reviewers made similarly confident predictions about the novel's future. The *New York Times* review "Three Lives in Supreme Torture: Mrs. Wharton's *Ethan Frome* a Cruel, Compelling, Haunting Story of New England" honors the author's artistry, suggesting that the contrivances of the slim plot would be hopelessly clumsy in lesser hands. This October 8 review praises the narrative structure of the work and judges it a significant advance for Wharton: "The author of *The House of Mirth,* which lacked much of being either a great novel or a true one, and which lacked also not a little of being a really convincing drama, in spite of the element of truth and the wide popular appeal which has caused it to stand forth in the popular mind as Mrs. Wharton's most conspicuous achievement, has accomplished in this story something very much finer and stronger" (Tuttleton 182). Uncertain about the classification of the work—long short story or short novel—the *New York Times* writer is certain nonetheless that it is "an impressive tragedy" (Tuttleton 182).

The October 26 *Nation* review recommends the novel in similarly strong language, finding in *Ethan Frome* the long awaited fulfillment of its author's early promise. "The wonder is that the spectacle of so much pain can be made to yield so much beauty," the reviewer notes in admiration (Tuttleton 184).

The British review which appeared in the January 1912 edition of *Bookman* echoes these same sentiments, announcing that "Mrs. Wharton has more than satisfied one's expectation, and her art has never been shown to greater advantage than in this story of Ethan Frome" (Tuttleton 186). Reviewers hesitant to treat Wharton as a major American writer after the publication of *The House of Mirth* in 1905 were convinced of her place in the literary tradition when they read *Ethan Frome*.

Some reviewers extended this recognition to Wharton in less flattering terms than others, perpetuating the misconception that she was a protégée of her friend James by heralding the new novel as evidence of an unexpectedly independent vision.[3] Eager to praise her work, the *Nation* reviewer introduces her as an imitator of James who has suddenly forged her own style: "Practiced, cosmopolitan, subtle, she has seemed, on the whole, to covet most earnestly the refinements of Henry James. In spite of her habit of a franker approach, her consistent rating of matter above manner, and the gravitation—we should hesitate to say transfer—of her interest from exotic to native themes; we might have been reasonably content to rank her as the greatest pupil of a little master, were it not for the appearance of *Ethan Frome*" (Tuttleton 183). The review which appeared in *Current Literature* pursues the same invidious comparison, opening with the announcement that with the writing of *Ethan Frome* Wharton has succeeded in freeing herself from "the thraldom of Henry James" (112). The reviewer continues by supplying another metaphor for this relationship between the two writers, "She has long been supposed, as the New York *Sun* puts it, to worship Henry James on her knees. Now, says that paper, she is standing on her feet" (112). The consensus that emerges from the three reviews—amidst strongly favorable reactions to the novel itself—is that Wharton is heavily indebted to James for her successes in fiction. Treating *Ethan Frome* as proof of her maturation as an artist, the writers never examine the assumption that she depended on James before 1911.

Another common theme of the 1911 reviews concerns the darkness of the novel's tone and situation. The *Independent* review comments on the power which Wharton derives from the situation of Ethan and Mattie, figures who experience "twenty-four years of hideous death in life" following forty-eight hours of passionate life (1204). For other writers, the bleakness of the ending overshadows all other considerations, including Wharton's craft. Her biographer R. W. B. Lewis cites an early library guide which describes the novel as "too pessimistic to be recommended to the general reader" (310). England's *Saturday Review* expresses a similar sentiment, despite prose which impresses the reviewer strongly: "The writing is singularly beautiful. It has passed through [the] flame of the author's imagination. Yet, having read the story, we wish we had not read it. The error is in the end. There are things too terrible in their failure to be told humanly by creature to creature" (Tuttleton 185). Contemplating the fate of Ethan and Mattie after the failure of their suicide attempt, the reviewer finds not nobility or tragedy but "exaggerated terror." The October 30 Hartford *Daily Courant* disparages the ending even more stridently, suggesting that what tragedy exists in *Ethan Frome* is "purely physical" rather than spiritual—"an unflinching tragedy of banalities, dyspepsia and spinal injury" (Tuttleton 185). Reviewing the novel for *Bookman*, Frederic Taber Cooper confesses that he finds the novel unforgivable for its "utter remorselessness." Torn like most reviewers between admiration for the author's narrative style and dismay over her choice of subject, Cooper concludes that the novel is "as perfect in technique as it is relentless in substance" (Tuttleton 186).

Approaching the novel as the work of an author who favors depictions of "life in its unsmiling aspects," the *New York Times* review inaugurates a major theme in *Ethan Frome* criticism by comparing Wharton to the ancient Greeks. Conceding that the fate of the romantic couple at novel's end is nothing less than "infinite refinement of torture," this reviewer treats the cruelty of the work as the inheritance of Greek tragedy. More specifically, he argues that Wharton has imbibed the "remorseless spirit of the Greek tragic muse," appropriating the vestiges of New England Puritanism as her surrogate for the Fates of classical literature (Tuttleton 181). This comparison of the novel to Greek tragedy shapes several other contemporary reviews (and a long line of critical essays as well). The British edition of *Bookman* views the novel as an "intensely human story" unfolding with the inexorability of Greek tragedy (Tuttleton 187). The *Nation* reviewer concludes by invoking the familiar image of the medusa head, drawing a strong parallel between the legendary figure and the nineteenth-century farmer.

There is possible, within the gamut of human experience, an exaltation of anguish which makes a solitude for itself, whose direct contemplation seals the impulse of speech and strikes cold upon the heart. Yet sometimes in reflection there is revealed, beneath the wringing torment, the lineaments of a wronged and distorted loveliness. It is the piteous and intolerable conception which the Greeks expressed in the medusa head that Mrs. Wharton has dared to hold up to us anew, but the face she shows us is the face of our own people. (Tuttleton 184–85)

From this perspective, Wharton's portrayal of the ruined lives left to Ethan and Mattie after the crash becomes an indictment of conditions in the remote villages of modern New England. The tragedy which she forces her readers to confront, the metaphorical medusa head, is the toll of living in a world which has lost its vitality and purpose.

Not all reviewers recognized—or accepted—the New England which figures so prominently in *Ethan Frome,* however. Writing for the *New Republic,* Elizabeth Shepley Sergeant emerged as the most persuasive of the contemporary writers questioning the authenticity of Wharton's New England. Her 1915 response to the novel is framed as a dialogue between two readers, one convinced that the work is a "landmark in American literature" and the other intent on championing the superior work of local color realists from the region (20). The speaker (Sergeant herself) is willing to acknowledge the author's artistry, but not her command of life in the Berkshires. The review thus challenges the novelist's claim to understand the life which she observed during her summers at the Mount, insisting that *Ethan Frome* fails to deal fairly with its subject. "Do Zeena's false teeth click true, do Ethan and Mattie make love in Starkfield fashion, would they have taken the fatal coast that brought about the intolerable horror of their lives?" (20). Developing this line of argument, Sergeant contrasts *Ethan Frome* to the fiction of Sarah Orne Jewett and Mary Wilkins Freeman. The latter writers, native New Englanders, impress the reviewer for their ability to render the complexity of life in their region by incorporating light as well as shadows. Dismissing *Ethan Frome* as a "literary copy" of the life captured so vividly by the local color realists, Sergeant concludes by predicting that Wharton's novel will fade from view long before the fiction of Jewett and Freeman.[4]

EARLY CRITICISM

Consideration of Wharton's achievement in *Ethan Frome* figures prominently in early evaluations of her art. Reviewers who hailed the novel as a masterpiece when it appeared in 1911 set the tone for much of the discourse which followed during Wharton's lifetime. Increasingly honored during the uneasy years between the world wars as "the foremost living American writer of fiction,"[5] Wharton became the focus of a significant number of critical studies examining the emergence of the modern novel. Although these works treat her many stories and novels of Old New York as more characteristic expressions of her style and vision, they repeatedly single out *Ethan Frome* as the greatest success of her career. Russell Blankenship's words of praise in his 1931 survey *American Literature as an Expression of the National Mind* convey the prevailing attitude toward the novel twenty years after its publication: "By general acclamation *Ethan Frome* (1911) has been declared Mrs. Wharton's masterpiece and one of the finest triumphs of all American literature.... The art of Mrs. Wharton is seen at its very finest in this story. Reducing the materials of the tragedy to the minimum and telling the story with a clipped spareness of phrase, the author achieves a powerful intensity that is excessively rare in our literature" (507). Proclaimed an American classic as early as 1911, the novel became required reading in high schools across the nation in Wharton's lifetime.[6]

The prominence which *Ethan Frome* achieved clearly influenced early attempts to determine Wharton's place in the American literary tradition. Set in a world far removed from the more familiar drawing rooms and country estates of her upbringing, the novel was her thirteenth book in fifteen years. Yet for many critics it was this short but powerful evocation of the lonely New England village which secured Wharton's reputation as a major American author. In his study *Contemporary American Novelists 1900–1920*, Carl Van Doren advances *Ethan Frome* as a novel worthy of Nathaniel Hawthorne. Analyzing the continuing pressure of circumstance on Wharton's characters and plots, he argues that her perspective as an outsider grants her a depth of understanding missing from the work of later New England writers. "Not since Hawthorne has a novelist built on the New England soil a tragedy of such elevation of mood as this. Freed from the bondage of local color, that myopic muse, Mrs. Wharton here handles her material not so much like a quarryman finding curious stones and calling out about them as like a sculptor setting up his finished work on a commanding hill" (99–100). Finding in *Ethan Frome* Wharton's most intense exploration of human passion, Van Doren identifies her with the greatest New England writer in American fiction.

For other critics, the novel is evidence of Wharton's affinity with naturalism rather than romanticism. Emphasizing the stricken lives of all three characters, Ralph Philip Boas and Katherine Burton point to the strength of the connection between Wharton and the naturalist writer Hamlin Garland. The experiences of "isolation and dreariness and bitter poverty" which dominate *Ethan Frome* are not confined to New England, they argue, but form the texture of life for Midwestern pioneers in Garland's *Main-Travelled Roads* as well (265). Edwin Bjorkman's work *Voices of To-Morrow: Critical Studies of the New Spirit in Literature* concentrates even more closely on the inescapable poverty of Wharton's characters and the barrenness of their lovely surroundings in the Berkshires. Praising the acuity of the author's vision, Bjorkman suggests that the tragedy which she presents is social rather than personal. She permits her characters no redemption, no release from their misery, because she seeks to expose prevailing conditions rather than improve them. "In doing this, and doing it with her usual exquisiteness of word and phrase and portraiture, Mrs. Wharton has passed from individual to social art; from the art that excites to that which incites," Bjorkman concludes (299).

Wharton's choice of subject matter provoked even more discussion than her social criticism. In a 1933 study of British and American fiction, E. K. Brown emphasizes the gap between *Ethan Frome* and all of Wharton's previous work: "Few books can have so surprised an author's public as did *Ethan Frome* in 1911. For more than a decade Mrs. Wharton's fiction had dealt exclusively with metropolitan and cosmopolitan society … with each passing year she had proved herself more and more the novelist of civilization; yet in *Ethan Frome* she accomplished something as bleak and simple as a sketch of Sarah Orne Jewett" (202). Wharton's fascination with the New England villages bordering her summer home at the Mount, evident in the 1917 novel *Summer* as well as in *Ethan Frome,* reassured other critics that she remained an American writer despite her removal to Europe in 1907.

Much of the criticism which appeared in the postwar period makes pointed reference to her expatriate status, even as it celebrates the Americanness of *Ethan Frome*. In his 1923 essay on Wharton, Percy Boynton treats the novel as the author's demonstration that she is capable of working with "undiluted American material" (29).

Such proof was obviously important to a number of critics and scholars seeking continuity between nineteenth- and twentieth-century American literature in a period governed by the experimentation of High Modernism. Boynton suggests that the death of William Dean Howells in 1920 made Wharton's role as intermediary between two literary generations all the more compelling. Robert Morss Lovett proceeds similarly in his 1925 study of Wharton, establishing the tensions and ideals of 1890s literary realism as an important context for her art. Treating *Ethan Frome* as her masterpiece, he approaches Wharton as an artist blandishing "the last enchantments of the Victorian age" (87). In his work *Main Currents in American Thought*, Vernon Parrington contends that the gap between Wharton and twentieth-century life is greater still; he praises *Ethan Frome* as her finest achievement, but aligns her with the ancien régime and calls her "the last of our literary aristocrats of the genteel tradition" (381, 382).

No consideration of Wharton's place in the literary tradition after 1911 is complete without reference to Henry James, at least according to the earliest essays and book-length studies devoted to her work. This criticism is founded on the lingering assumption that Wharton learned her craft from the Master and began her career by imitating his style and adopting his choice of subjects. The view of Wharton espoused in most of the book reviews— relegating her to the status of "the greatest pupil of a little master"—is merely embellished more fully in longer discussions of *Ethan Frome*. The first chapter of Lovett's book on Wharton, for example, concentrates not on her but on James. Boynton's essay begins by noting the signs of his influence on her fiction, and Van Doren's discussion ends by terming him "her principal master in fiction" (103). This identification of Wharton as James's student endured for several decades following her death in 1937. In his 1932 study of the twentieth-century novel, Joseph Warren Beach praises *Ethan Frome* as Wharton's unique achievement of "a simple and tragic realism which can stand comparison with almost anything in fiction" (311). However, he insists that the novel's point of view—an enduring source of pride for Wharton—is merely an application of Jamesian technique (293–94). Examining Wharton's fiction in his book *The Novel in English* (1931), Grant C. Knight finds evidence of James's tutelage in every work but one. *Ethan Frome* is the novel which Knight describes as Wharton's masterpiece, an American classic which represents her only "escape from [James's] domination" (334).

In 1938 the British critic Q. D. Leavis published a more insightful analysis of Wharton's standing, albeit under the title "Henry James' Heiress: The

Importance of Edith Wharton" (1938). In this essay of general appreciation, Leavis passes quickly over the lesser fiction of the last decade of the author's life in order to champion the work of lasting value. Describing Wharton as "combined social critic and historian," Leavis argues the excellence of the earlier New York novels and New England stories (194). Leavis compares Wharton the ironist to James, but also to Jane Austen and (especially) George Eliot. Further, the essay challenges the widely held view of Wharton as mere follower of James by pressing a vital distinction between the two: "The American novel grew up with Henry James and achieved a tradition with Mrs. Wharton" (196). Pointing to James's increasingly tenuous grasp of twentieth-century American life, the critic praises Wharton's superior ability to portray a society in flux in novels such as *The House of Mirth* and *The Custom of the Country*. Although she considers the latter to be Wharton's masterpiece, Leavis admires *Ethan Frome* and considers it another illustration of the author's developed understanding of social conditions in modern America. Calling Wharton's New England fiction "informed realism," Leavis advances both *Ethan Frome* and *Summer* as works which give the lie to earlier, sentimental depictions of the countryside (204).

In the closing decade of Wharton's life, discussion of *Ethan Frome* continued to flourish on this side of the Atlantic. The novel loomed large in overviews of the author's career, of course, but it also inspired more focused analysis in a number of books and essays. The question of the novel's form remained central for most. Van Meter Ames' 1928 study, *The Aesthetics of the Novel*, holds up *Ethan Frome* as an exemplar of structure in modern fiction. In his chapter devoted to technique, Ames cites the prevailing view of Wharton as "the most careful craftsman among present American writers" and details the effectiveness of the frame device in place in *Ethan Frome* (187). A measure of his esteem for the novel is his contention that it recalls Gustave Flaubert's *Madame Bovary* in its economy and its subtlety. Fred Lewis Pattee's 1930 survey, *The New American Literature: 1890–1930*, endorses the widespread view that *Ethan Frome* is Wharton's best work but argues that it is too narrowly intellectual. Finding the novel perfect artistically, Pattee nonetheless presses the point that Wharton's fiction lacks spirit (253).

Two important essays devoted to the question of Wharton's technique in *Ethan Frome* completed this early period of criticism. Poet and critic John Crowe Ransom explores the implications of the novel's point of view in "Characters and Character: A Note on Fiction," an essay published in a 1936 volume of *American Review*. Acknowledging the difficulty which Wharton faced as she sought the proper narrator for Ethan's story,[7] Ransom compares the "special reporter" which she created to similar figures in the modern novels of James, Joseph Conrad and Willa Cather (272–73). Ransom's analysis of the effectiveness of Wharton's visiting engineer is set against a variety of post-Victorian narrative approaches. Noting the great gap between Wharton's experience and that of her inarticulate farmer, Ransom argues that the novel fails to illuminate Ethan's inner life to any satisfactory degree.

Bernard DeVoto reaches a similar conclusion in his introduction to the 1938 edition of the novel, presenting the work as a hollow triumph of "sheer story" (xvii). His starting point is the established view of the novel as Wharton's best, a judgment which he attributes to her technical prowess. Entering the continuing debate over the authenticity of Wharton's New England, DeVoto finds the setting and its characters a literary construct only. Jewett or Freeman would have breathed life into daily experiences which Wharton never understood, he contends. The technical merits of the novel are impressive but finally insufficient for DeVoto: "*Ethan Frome* is a model of literary technique but it is not a transcript of human experience; it is a 'well-made' novel done with exact calculation and superb skill, but it is not an exploration of or comment on genuine emotion. It is, in short, literally a masterpiece, an exhibition of flawless craftsmanship by a writer who has learned all there is to learn about her trade" (vi). Arguing the limits of the narrative detachment cultivated first by Flaubert and then by James, DeVoto points to the consequence in *Ethan Frome*. The novel offers "magnificent story-telling" but not felt life, superb craftsmanship but not human sympathy (xvii–xviii).

DRAMATIC SUCCESS

In the last few years of Wharton's life, *Ethan Frome* made unexpected gains with the reading public. Originally a greater popular success in England than America, the novel enjoyed rising sales during the years of the Great Depression and became a "perennial seller" by the early 1940s (Lewis 3). One reason for this surge in interest was a 1936 adaptation of the novel by the Pulitzer Prize winner Owen Davis and his son Donald. Pleased by the literate quality of their script, Wharton agreed to supply the Foreword for their text. After expressing her thorough satisfaction with the Davises' translation of Ethan and Mattie to the stage, Wharton uses the occasion to comment on her most famous novel a quarter century after she completed it.

I should like to record here my appreciation of this unusual achievement, and my professional admiration for the great skill and exquisite sensitiveness with which my interpreters have executed their task; ... [if the actors also succeed] then my poor little group of hungry lonely New England villagers will live again for a while on their stony hillside before finally joining their forbears under the village head-stones. I should like to think that this good fortune may be theirs, for I lived among them, in fact and in imagination, for more than ten years, and their strained starved faces are still near to me. (viii)

With these closing words, Wharton reasserts her familiarity with the landscape of Starkfield (a point of contention since 1911) and acknowledges an imaginative preoccupation with its inhabitants.

Wharton's claim of lingering concern for her characters is borne out by the number of times she refused to entertain requests to adapt the novel. Protective of the novel for more than two decades, she rebuffed a series of producers and playwrights attracted by the dramatic qualities of the work. By the mid-1930s, however, she had fresh reasons to consider mounting a theatrical production of *Ethan Frome*. Reliant on her pen to support herself and more than two dozen dependents,[8] Wharton watched her royalties dwindle during the early years of the Great Depression. Disappointed by the sales figures for her autobiography *A Backward Glance* (1934), Wharton began to seek new sources of income first in Hollywood and then on Broadway. She was receptive when two emerging film studios approached her for the rights to *Ethan Frome*, for she thought the novel ideal for filming (Benstock 438). When producers began to express concern over the grimness of the ending—wondering how many Depression-era moviegoers would find the story entertaining—negotiations for the rights faltered and were eventually abandoned. Although Wharton earned more than $50,000 by selling the rights to other novels (*The Age of Innocence, The Children*), *Ethan Frome* would not be filmed until 1993.[9]

The novel's progress to the stage began in California in 1934, when the son of a Santa Barbara theatre manager attempted his own adaptation under the name "Lowell Barrington" and mailed the result to a New York producer ("Owen Davis & Son Help 'Ethan Frome' " 33). Impressed by the script, the producer Jed Harris forwarded it to Wharton in France. She agreed to a theatrical production, but stipulated that the producer needed to secure the services of Davis, "that man who wrote *Icebound*" ("Owen Davis & Son Help 'Ethan Frome' " 33). Wharton had more than one reason to be optimistic about an adaptation of *Ethan Frome* at this time. She had confidence in her choice of playwright to rewrite the Barrington adaptation, for she knew and admired Davis' 1923 drama about rural New England. Also, she was already savoring the great success of a theatrical version of her novella *Old Maid*. That play opened on Broadway at the start of 1935, won the year's Pulitzer's Prize and continued to draw large audiences as it toured. The Davis adaptation of *Ethan Frome* debuted in Philadelphia in January 1936 and began a long run at the National Theatre in New York two weeks later. Buoyed by the popular response to these works on stage, Wharton began writing a play named *Kate Spain* which was inspired by the story of Lizzie Borden. Worsening health prevented her from completing her own dramatic effort, but the revenue from the adaptations of *The Old Maid* and *Ethan Frome* (totaling approximately $130,000) eased her financial burdens significantly (Lewis 529). Learning of plans to stage *Ethan Frome* in England, in March 1936 Wharton crowed to a friend, "It seems so funny to be blazing along several Great White Ways at a time, and I only wish the tax-collectors of both hemispheres would look the other way" (qtd. in Benstock 446).

The reviews of the Davis adaptation were also deeply gratifying. Again and again, the praise which contemporary writers lavished on the New York production was extended even more enthusiastically to the novel. The theatre reviews commend aspects of stagecraft such as the bare sets defining the Frome household and the representation of the climactic sledding accident. They also emphasize the strength of the performances by Raymond Massey (Ethan), Pauline Lord (Zeena) and Ruth Gordon (Mattie). At the center of most play reviews, however, are powerful reminders of Wharton's achievement in the novel, with writers reaffirming the centrality of her "frosty little masterpiece" ("New Plays in Manhattan" 25) and predicting that the work will have the longest reach of all her fiction ("The Play and Screen" 414). Critics of the play linger over the inherently dramatic quality of Wharton's narrative, pointing to the "sculpturally simple outlines of the novel" ("Ethan Frome" 167) and emphasizing the tragic dimension of the work.

Mrs. Wharton drew with austere economy a picture of three descendants of the Pilgrims, caught in a trap of their own steel discipline: Ethan who married Zenia (*sic*) for fear the winter might sap his sanity as it had his mother's; Zenia, sterile and ingrown who makes romance for herself out of her own ailments; Mattie, like a frail anemone on the rocks, looking for love and sunlight and giving them freely. What escape could there be for Ethan and Mattie when Zenia brought Mattie to live with her? . . . There have been few tragedies so apparently inevitable and conclusive. (Wyatt 723)

These words of praise suggest how the 1936 play reinvigorated discussions of the 1911 novel. Wharton received fresh evidence of her novel's vitality and appeal one year before her death, and twenty-six years after the publication of *Ethan Frome*.

7

BIBLIOGRAPHIC ESSAY

By the late 1920s, *Ethan Frome* was firmly established in American letters as the pinnacle of Edith Wharton's artistic achievement. The author herself held a different view of the novel, and she expressed her impatience with its reputation in a 1933 essay: "I am far from thinking *Ethan Frome* my best novel, and I am bored and even exasperated when I am told that it is" (391).[1] Her exasperation did nothing to temper enthusiasm for the work in the years before her death in 1937, and *Ethan Frome* continued to absorb the attention of Wharton critics and scholars through the 1970s. Certain questions which organized early discussions of the novel, such as the authenticity of the New England setting or the influence of Henry James, provoked debate even as new issues took shape.[2] By the start of the 1980s, however, the growing dominance of feminist theory in Wharton studies signaled a waning of interest in *Ethan Frome*. Over the past twenty-five years, the attention of scholars has shifted to novels of Old New York, particularly *The House of Mirth* and *The Custom of the Country*, and to previously neglected works such as *The Reef*. *The House of Mirth* has become the focus of more recent criticism than any other Wharton novel. *Ethan Frome* remains an important novel in the author's oeuvre, but it is no longer regarded as her masterpiece.

HISTORICAL CRITICS

Scholarly interest in *Ethan Frome* since Wharton's death can be divided into three broad categories. The first is composed of critics who wrote in the

1940s and 1950s on the historical and political implications of the work. Edmund Wilson's essay "Justice to Edith Wharton" is a noteworthy example. Published in his 1941 collection *The Wound and the Bow*, the essay was inspired by Wilson's dissatisfaction with the Wharton obituaries which underestimated her importance during the years 1905–1917. Honoring her as a "passionate social prophet" of American literature (160), Wilson argues that *Ethan Frome* was not an oddity in her career but an extension of her concern with the world of privilege: "It is true that she knew the top strata better than she knew anything else; but both in *The House of Mirth* and *The Fruit of the Tree*, she is always aware of the pit of misery which is implied by the wastefulness of the plutocracy, and the horror or the fear of this pit is one of the forces that determines the action" (165). Alfred Kazin's 1942 study *On Native Grounds* devotes a chapter to the fiction of Wharton and Theodore Dreiser and reaches a strikingly different conclusion about her depiction of poverty in *Ethan Frome*. "The world of the Frome tragedy is abstract," Kazin insists (60). Treating Wharton's art as inferior to Dreiser's as well as James's, Kazin contends that her patrician upbringing thwarted her efforts to understand—or even imagine—the poor of New England or London or Paris.

Other works published in this period examine the texture of Wharton's New England, continuing a discussion begun in the earliest reviews of the novel. Nancy R. Leach's essay "New England in the Stories of Edith Wharton," published in a 1957 issue of *The New England Quarterly*, surveys three fragmentary novels found among Wharton's unpublished papers at Yale in an attempt to determine her standing as a regional writer. Setting *Ethan Frome* in the context of Wharton's New England fiction, Leach finds occasional errors of detail or dialect,[3] but praises the author's understanding of modern life in villages which are defined by "their lack of culture and economic opportunity, rapidly being depopulated by the more ambitious and talented young people, and serving instead as a refuge for old people and those defeated in spirit" (96). Abigail Hamblen's later paper "Edith Wharton in New England" is more critical of the author's depiction of the region in *Ethan Frome* and *Summer*. Contrasting Wharton to native local colorists, Hamblen criticizes the Romantic glorification of nature over society in *Ethan Frome* and concludes that the novel's portrayal of the region is actually "New England seen from a distance" (244).

In 1953 Blake Nevius published his study *Edith Wharton*, the most perceptive of the early volumes devoted to the author's work. Tracing the underlying continuity of Wharton's fiction, he explores the implications of two recurring situations or themes: the generous nature trapped by circumstance in a relationship with a meaner figure, and the limits of individual responsibility within the larger society (9–10). In his chapter on *Ethan Frome*, Nevius discusses the title character's sense of duty as a vestige of Puritanism dooming the farmer to "a life of sterile expiation" (121). W. D. MacCallan's 1952 publication of the novel's beginnings, the French copy book exercise which Wharton wrote in 1907, marked another important contribution to Wharton scholarship. "The French Draft of *Ethan Frome*" provides the complete text of the original sketch and a summary of the editing which Wharton and her tutor attempted. Although a translation of this French version still needs to be prepared, MacCallan's essay offers a good overview of the chief differences between the 1907 exercise and the 1911 novel.[4]

The single most important essay written on *Ethan Frome* appeared in 1956, when Lionel Trilling was invited to discuss the novel in a series of lectures entitled "The Literary Presentations of Great Moral Issues." Not the best of Trilling's work, and certainly not the best of *Frome* criticism, "The Morality of Inertia" nonetheless quelled debate for years. Trilling approaches the work as "a mere accident of American culture" (31), ascribing its stature to the mistaken American assumption that pessimism is more truthful than optimism. Claiming that Wharton inflicts gratuitous cruelty upon her three characters, he attempts to cite Aristotle's theory of tragedy as evidence of the novel's failure. The work raises no moral issue, Trilling argues, for the protagonist never makes a choice. The critic finds only one worthwhile idea in *Ethan Frome*: "The idea is this: that moral inertia, the *not* making of moral decisions, constitutes a large part of the moral life of humanity" (37). Mistaking moral inertia for *tradition*, Trilling patronizes *Ethan Frome* (as well as the Book of Job) for portraying ordinary men and women who discharge "the dull, unthinking round of duties" assigned to them (40).[5]

NEW CRITICS AND SCHOLARS

The first publications to follow "The Morality of Inertia" appeared in the 1960s, as New Critics turned to the novel. Ceding moral questions to Trilling, several of these papers concentrate on *Ethan Frome*'s unity of image and symbol. Marius Bewley's neglected review essay "Mrs. Wharton's Mask" (1964) is a striking exception, for it challenges the central premise of Trilling's argument. Written on the occasion of Scribner's reissue of *A Backward Glance, Summer* and *Old New York*, Bewley's essay attempts to restore *Ethan Frome* to its former prominence among Wharton's works. Contending that *Ethan Frome* is a "moral parable," Bewley offers a reading of the work which emphasizes the two important decisions which the protagonist makes as the climax approaches. Wharton's protagonist is not morally passive, Bewley asserts, and the misery which he endures for years is the consequence of his decision to take his life. "The horrifying closing scene in the kitchen in which Ethan, Mattie, and Zeena seem to confront one another forever is not suffering wantonly imposed on her characters by an embittered female writer, but a punishment that grows ineluctably out of a moral action deliberately performed, and the punishment is meant to exist as an evaluation of that action" (8). For Bewley, the novel enjoys the stature of Wharton's masterpieces *The House of Mirth* and *The Custom of the Country*.

Bewley's argument rebutting "The Morality of Inertia" in Trilling's own terms supplies a valuable context for the work of New Critics pursuing formal and technical matters. Kenneth Bernard's 1961 paper "Imagery and Symbolism in *Ethan Frome*" attributes to the novel "a stylistic and organizational brilliance" (178) and suggests that its imagery is a vital guide to meaning. For evidence, Bernard points to the emphasis which Wharton places on setting, light and dark imagery and sexual symbolism. Joseph X. Brennan's "*Ethan Frome*: Structure and Metaphor" is a valuable study of the way the novel's chief metaphors develop the character of the narrator. Brennan works particularly closely with the shaping contrasts of the work, exploring how they influence tone. In the essay "Circularity: Theme and Structure in *Ethan Frome*," Charles Bruce establishes the symmetry of the novel's prologue and epilogue, arguing that the pattern is intended to convey the sheer monotony of the characters' lives.

Two essays from 1977 argue that the novel is more complex than previous critics acknowledged. In "The Ordered Disorder of *Ethan Frome*," David Eggenschwiler disputes the conclusions of Bernard as well as Trilling, insisting on the prevailing ambiguity of the work. Tracing Wharton's uses of irony, Eggenschwiler finds a deeply ambivalent protagonist and a "coherent and complex novel" (245). Alan Henry Rose's paper "'Such Depths of Sad Initiation': Edith Wharton and New England" analyzes *Ethan Frome* in the context of *Summer* and earlier short stories set in the region. Emphasizing the "dark extremes" which distinguish Wharton's New England fiction from her New York novels (423), Rose treats the failure which defines Ethan's life as the reflection of a barren culture.

The 1975 publication of R. W. B. Lewis' biography of Wharton marked another advance in *Frome* scholarship. Lewis places the novel in the American literary tradition of Hawthorne and Melville, examining resonances of their work in Wharton's story of Starkfield. Evoking the different pressures on Wharton as she wrote *Ethan Frome*—the waning of her affair with Morton Fullerton and the worsening condition of Teddy Wharton—Lewis also sheds fresh light on the sources of the novel's intensity. Cynthia Griffin Wolff's biography *A Feast of Words: The Triumph of Edith Wharton*, published two years later, takes a psychoanalytical approach to the woman and her work. In her extended discussion of *Ethan Frome*, Wolff claims that the narrator is Wharton's center of interest and the entire narrative his "dream vision" (161) of the wintry life he might have led. Although Shari Benstock's 1994 biography *No Gifts from Chance* clarifies aspects of Wharton's relationship with Fullerton, a question of considerable importance for *Ethan Frome*, Lewis' biography remains the definitive work.[6]

THEORETICAL CRITICS

By the start of the 1980s, discussion of the novel took a more theoretical turn. Although Wharton's other novels began to attract a range of contemporary approaches including deconstruction and cultural criticism, *Ethan Frome* became the province of feminist criticism almost exclusively.[7] Wolff's interpretation of Ethan's story as a projection of the narrator's deepest fears provoked a number of responses at the start of the decade. Elizabeth Ammons' 1980 work *Edith Wharton's Argument with America* attempts to explore the mythical roots of the author's fiction, treating *Ethan Frome* as a fairy tale which indicts society.[8] The moral which the critic extracts— "fairy-tale visions of love and marriage imprison rather than liberate men and women" (61)—is dependent on the visiting engineer who imagines the story. According to Ammons, this narrator shares with his subject a deep-seated fear of woman as witch.

Two additional works which approach Ethan's story as the narrator's dream are Wendy Gimbel's *Edith Wharton: Orphancy and Survival* (1984) and Judith Fryer's *Felicitous Space: The Imaginative Structures of Edith Wharton and Willa Cather* (1986).[9] In Gimbel's interpretation, the startling features of the Frome house prompt the narrator to imagine a story which unfolds in a "symbolic dimension of human experience" (64). The principles of literary realism are jettisoned, and Mattie and Ethan are transformed into children trapped in their mother's dark house. Concentrating on women's space in fiction, Fryer's study offers a more persuasive discussion of the Frome house and its influence. She attends closely to the design of the nineteenth-century New England farmhouse, pointing out the ways the misshapen Frome house represents a subversion of the original plan (189).

R. B. Hovey's 1986 essay "*Ethan Frome*: A Controversy about Modernizing It" challenges Wolff's and Ammons' interpretations of the novel, arguing that the two critics "reshape Wharton's art almost beyond recognition" (4). Disputing the conclusions which they reach, Hovey points out the danger of relying on abstractions in literary criticism. His paper includes a valuable critique of Wolff's and Ammons' view of love in Wharton's fiction: "Both critics eliminate from even the ideal of love the *caritas* which affirmative *Eros* has included as far back as Ruth of the Old Testament: that supposedly each lover, man or woman, has wished to serve, to do for, the beloved. By contrast, the love-ethic these critics apply to *Ethan Frome* is self-assertion, self-fulfillment. They write like, if not champions, surely products of what has been labeled 'the Culture of Narcissism'" (18). For Hovey, the consequence of this approach is a failure to recognize either the novel's tragic implications or the complexity of its moral issues.

The doomed lovers of the novel continued to provoke discussion through the decade. Carol Wershoven's work *The Female Intruder in the Novels of Edith Wharton* (1982) traces a recurring character type in the author's fiction, a young woman positioned on the fringes of a hostile society. Wershoven advances Mattie Silver as the best example of this figure, "the woman who is at once more vital, braver, and more receptive to all of life than the society she must confront and challenge" (22). Jean Frantz Blackall's essay "The Sledding Accident in Ethan Frome" (1984) discusses Ethan's protectiveness toward Mattie at the top of School House Hill. It also sheds light on the 1904 coasting accident in Lenox which inspired Wharton's choice of climax. Blackall's later paper "Edith Wharton's Art of Ellipses" analyzes the author's punctuation, arguing that the ellipses which frame Ethan's story serve as an "instrument of intensification" (155) intended to convey years of unending misery. Orlene Murad's essay "Edith Wharton and Ethan Frome" (1983) posits a "biological tie" (90) between author and protagonist so strong as to account for the disappearance of the first-person narrator from the novel. Trapped in her own unfulfilling marriage as she wrote the novel, Wharton assumed the role of the third-person narrator who tells the story of Ethan's abortive romance with Mattie.

Other works from this period have less value for students of the novel than they do for students of theory or social change. Josephine Donovan's study *After the Fall* (1989) attempts to argue the centrality of the Demeter-Persephone myth in Wharton's fiction, describing the "fundamental subtext" of the author's work as "the luring of the daughters out of their mothers' gardens into the patriarchal symbolic" (49). Casting Wharton's disapproval of New England local colorists as a rejection of the feminine and the maternal, Donovan reads *Ethan Frome* as the story of Demeter's revenge. Candace Waid's *Edith Wharton's Letters from the Underworld* (1991) also makes prominent use of the Persephone myth, interpreting the author's major works as tracts on women and the act of writing. For Waid, *Ethan Frome* is Wharton's sustained contemplation of "the prison of inarticulateness" (62).

Although the pace of *Frome* criticism has continued to slow, two books published in the 1990s deserve attention. Donna M. Campbell's *Resisting Regionalism* traces the late nineteenth-century shift in American fiction from "feminine" local color realism to "masculine" naturalism, arguing the influence of regional writing on Crane, Norris and Dreiser. Treating Wharton's fiction as a "fusion" of local color and naturalism, Campbell offers an insightful analysis of the ways in which *Ethan Frome*'s modern narrator criticizes "standard local color myths" such as an organic community, the possibility of healing and the experience of renunciation (168). Carol J. Singley's *Edith Wharton: Matters of Mind and Spirit* (1995) is another carefully researched study, distinguished by its persuasive examination of the artist's developing religious and philosophical views. Describing *Ethan Frome* as Wharton's "most Calvinist [work]" (107), Singley places the novel in the tradition of Jonathan Edwards and Nathaniel Hawthorne and traces the influence of *The Scarlet Letter* on it. Emphasizing the greater bleakness of the 1911 novel, Singley contends that the work achieves a union of Calvinist belief and modernist aesthetic.

SECONDARY WORKS

Students of the novel will find a number of excellent resources available to them. Since the 1980s, the Edith Wharton Society has published a series of bibliographic essays which reflect the changing patterns in *Frome* criticism.[10] Kristin O. Lauer and Margaret P. Murray's 1990 volume *Edith Wharton: An Annotated Secondary Bibliography* is the most comprehensive reference to Wharton scholarship at this time. The 1992 work *Edith Wharton: The Contemporary Reviews*, edited by James Tuttleton, Lauer and Murray, includes a valuable array of *Frome* reviews from the years 1911–1915. Helen Killoran's *The Critical Reception of Edith Wharton* (2001) devotes a chapter to the novel under the expressive heading "The Murder of a Masterpiece." The Norton Critical Edition of the novel prepared by Lauer and Wolff serves as a helpful introduction to *Frome* secondary sources.

NOTES

INTRODUCTION

1. This appendix features scathing "reviews" from a variety of New York and London publications. The remarks attributed to *The Nation* are representative: "It is a false charity to reader and writer to mince matters. The English of it is that every character is a failure, the plot a vacuum, the style spiritless, the dialogue vague, the sentiment weak and the whole thing a fiasco." Lewis argues that Edith's dismissive reviews of her first effort at satire, though witty, reflect a habitual distrust of her own powers as a writer (31).

2. The other death Wharton is recalling here is that of her close friend Walter Berry. Weakened by appendicitis in 1926, he suffered two strokes in the following year and died on October 12, 1927. On the day of his death, Wharton wrote in her notebook, "The Love of all my life died today, and I with him" (Wolff 371).

3. Lewis and Wolff treat this stay in Philadelphia as a period of convalescence following a nervous breakdown. Both biographers report that Wharton spent months in Philadelphia under the care of S. Weir Mitchell, a doctor noted for his development of a controversial rest cure for neurasthenia. However, Benstock argues that Wharton neither suffered a breakdown nor sought Dr. Mitchell's help. The writer stayed in a suite of rooms at the Stenton Hotel, working on her fiction and corresponding regularly with Berry and other friends. The doctor was absent from Philadelphia for the whole of her visit, traveling to Turkey and Egypt in the aftermath of his daughter's death (Benstock 93–97).

4. In the chapter devoted to James in her autobiography, Wharton offers incisive analysis of her friend's late work. "I was naturally much interested in James's technical theories and experiments, though I thought, and still think, that he tended to sacrifice to them that spontaneity which is the life of fiction. . . . His latest novels, for all their

profound moral beauty, seemed to me more and more severed from that thick nourishing human air in which we all live and move. The characters in 'The Wings of the Dove' and 'The Golden Bowl' seem isolated in a Crookes tube for our inspection" (190).

CHAPTER 1.   CONTENT

1. All parenthetical citations refer to the Library of America edition of *Ethan Frome, Novellas and Other Writings* (New York, 1990).

CHAPTER 2.   TEXTS

1. The *Berkshire Evening Eagle*'s report of this fatal accident, published on March 12, 1904, may be found in the Norton Critical Edition of the novel. Lewis' biography also discusses this event and its influence on Wharton.

2. W. D. MacCallan's 1952 essay "The French Draft of *Ethan Frome*" supplies the copy book exercise, along with comments on the caliber of Wharton's written French. MacCallan also provides a helpful overview of the similarities between the 1907 sketch and the 1911 novel.

3. Wolff argues that this continuing interest on Wharton's part sets the novel apart from all other works in the author's oeuvre. Wolff comments on the preface to the dramatization in the following way: "Wharton was seventy-four when she wrote these words (just a little less than a year before her death), and there is a sense of insistent presence attached to the people of Starkfield that does not emerge when she refers to any other of her fictional creations" (155).

4. This revealing journal was published by Kenneth M. Price and Phyllis McBride in 1994. Their analysis of the Love Diary's language and tone is helpful to students of the novel.

CHAPTER 3.   CONTEXTS

1. Carol J. Singley treats *Ethan Frome* as an "important milestone" in Wharton's emerging career, noting that the dazzling success of *The House of Mirth* in 1905 was offset by the much weaker popular and critical response to *The Fruit of the Tree* in 1907. In her work *Edith Wharton: Matters of Mind and Spirit*, Singley argues that it was the novel *Ethan Frome* that secured Wharton's reputation (109).

2. Barbara White suggests that the force of Wharton's response to such criticism is a measure of her attachment to her New England fiction. White adds, "Wharton seldom responded to negative reviews, but she was stung by criticisms that she was an outsider who knew nothing of New England" (viii).

3. Wharton offers one of her fuller statements on the lingering effects of Puritanism in American society in her 1919 work, *French Ways and Their Meaning*. Commenting on the equality between men and women which distinguishes French society from American society, Wharton concludes, "The long hypocrisy which Puritan England handed on to America concerning the danger of frank and free social relations between men and women has done more than anything else to retard real civilization in America" (112–13).

4. Arguing that Ethan Frome owes more to *The Scarlet Letter* than "Ethan Brand" or *The Blithedale Romance*, Singley compares the red gash on Frome's forehead ("his badge of ignominy") to the embroidered "A" which Hester Prynne wears (113).

5. The novel also drew famous praise in 1925 from an admiring Willa Cather. She concludes her preface to the volume *The Best Stories of Sarah Orne Jewett* with the following evaluation: "If I were asked to name three American books which have the possibility of a long, long life, I would say at once, "The Scarlet Letter," "Huckleberry Finn," and "The Country of the Pointed Firs." I can think of no others that confront time and change so serenely" (xviii).

CHAPTER 4.   IDEAS

1. Zola's triumphant description of his first novel (*Therese Raquin*, 1867) captures the sweeping changes which he wished to effect: "I chose characters completely dominated by their nerves and their blood, deprived of free will, pushed to each action of their lives by the fatality of their flesh" (Mitchell 525). He demonstrated his confidence in these principles in his major achievement, a series of twenty novels devoted to the struggles of the Rougon-Macquart family during France's Second Empire. The novels demonstrate the inescapable forces of heredity and environment on Zola's most famous characters.

2. Dreiser's description of the individual in *Sister Carrie* remains a classic statement of American naturalism: "Among the forces which sweep and play throughout the universe, untutored man is but a wisp in the wind. Our civilization is still in a middle stage, scarcely beast, in that it is no longer wholly guided by instinct; scarcely human, in that it is not yet wholly guided by reason. On the tiger no responsibility rests. We see him aligned by nature with the forces of life—he is born into their keeping and without thought he is protected. We see man far removed from the lairs of the jungles, his innate instincts dulled by too near an approach to free will, his free will not sufficiently developed to replace his instincts and afford him perfect guidance. He is becoming too wise to hearken always to instincts and desires; he is still too weak to always prevail against them. As a beast, the forces of life aligned him with them; as a man, he has not yet wholly learned to align himself with the forces. In this intermediate stage he wavers—neither drawn in harmony with nature by his instincts nor yet wisely putting himself into harmony by his own free will. He is even as a wisp in the wind, moved by every breath of passion, acting now by his will and now by his instincts, erring with one, only to retrieve by the other, falling by one, only to rise by the other—a creature of incalculable variability" (70).

3. The inscription which Crane wrote on Hamlin Garland's copy of *Maggie* makes this concern explicit: "It is inevitable that you will be greatly shocked by this book but continue please with all possible courage to the end. For it tries to show that environment is a tremendous thing in the world and frequently shapes lives regardless. If one proves that theory one makes room in Heaven for all sorts of souls (notably an occasional street girl) who are not confidently expected to be there by many excellent people" (March 1893).

4. In his work *Social Darwinism in American Thought*, Richard Hofstadter describes the United States as "*the* Darwinian country": "American scientists were

prompt not only to accept the principle of natural selection but also to make important contributions to evolutionary science. The enlightened American reading public, which became fascinated with evolutionary speculation soon after the Civil War, gave a handsome reception to philosophies and political theories built in part upon Darwinism or associated with it. Herbert Spencer, who of all men made the most ambitious attempt to systematize the implications of evolution in fields other than biology itself, was far more popular in the United States than he was in his native country" (5). Hofstadter adds that Americans purchased 368,755 books by Spencer from the 1860s through 1903, "a figure probably unparalleled in such difficult spheres as philosophy and sociology" (34).

5. Cecelia Tichi's essay "Emerson, Darwin, and *The Custom of the Country*" is particularly helpful, exploring the separate influences of Darwin and Spencer on Wharton's major fiction. Noting the author's familiarity with the theories of both figures, Tichi argues the additional influence of Emerson on the "scheme of bifurcation" at the center of Wharton's major fiction: "The Emerson-Darwin nexus nonetheless provided Wharton the scheme of bifurcation by which to expose the crisis of sundered culture, which was the very crisis explored in her first major (and best-selling) novel, *The House of Mirth*, in which readers encountered a story line focused on the lethal social dislocations of aggressive new American wealth invading the traditional territory of landed gentry" (93).

6. In his introduction to *American Naturalism*, Harold Bloom cites the setting of *Ethan Frome* as "a world where the will is impotent, and tragedy is always circumstantial" (15).

7. Carol Singley contends that the novel's bleakness is shaped as much by Wharton's lingering Calvinism as by social Darwinism. In her work *Edith Wharton: Matters of Mind and Spirit*, Singley treats the recurrence of pain and suffering in Wharton's fiction as "remnants of her Calvinist sense of a punishing God." Singley comments, "Finally, it is tempting to think of Wharton's emphasis on human pain and suffering only in terms of scientific naturalism, but it is, in fact, a determinism born equally of a harsh theology as well as science. Upper-class Victorian culture, obsessed with material comfort, avoided pain and the nettling questions of individual moral responsibility as much as possible. Wharton, in contrast, adopts a more Calvinist creed. She lets her characters suffer and makes them individually accountable, even if they rarely have power to effect change in themselves or others" (65–66).

8. This same figure recurs in the fiction of Henry James, though James's spectators are put to different uses than Wharton's. As Tony Tanner suggests, the fate of the Jamesian spectator is most often exclusion or renunciation: "The intimate connection between comprehensiveness of vision and renunciation of participation is discernible in James's work almost from the first" (306).

9. J. X. Brennan treats this cat as the "watchful surrogate" of Zeena: "In its cunning, cruelty, and languid domesticity the cat indeed is the perfect representative of its mistress" (353).

10. In their work *No Man's Land*, Sandra M. Gilbert and Susan Gubar argue that the ironic contrast between Hawthorne's Zenobia and Wharton's Zeena illuminates *Ethan Frome*'s criticism of the limitations placed on nineteenth-century women. They comment, "Thus, though Wharton does not explicitly examine 'the woman question' in *Ethan Frome*, her novel implicitly points to an issue which concerned many of her

contemporaries: the issue of what women could realistically expect to attain and at what cost. Significantly, as the hope for a new future merged with revulsion against a contaminated past, and as the vision of a New Woman fused with horror at the traditional woman, much female-authored literature oscillated between extremes of exuberance and despair, between dreams of miraculous victory and nightmares of violent defeat" (81).

11. Wharton's imaginative interest in this situation persisted to the end of her career, but her writing during and after World War I took on a different character. The common predicament of heroines in her prewar fiction (1905–1912) remains notable.

12. Wharton underscores this point in Chapter VII, as Ethan considers Mattie's prospects: "Despair seized him at the thought of her setting out alone to renew the weary quest for work. In the only place where she was known she was surrounded by indifference or animosity; and what chance had she, inexperienced and untrained, among the million bread-seekers of the cities? There came back to him miserable tales he had heard at Worcester, and faces of girls whose lives had begun as hopefully as Mattie's.... It was not possible to think of such things without a revolt of his whole being. He sprang up suddenly" (50). Wharton herself learned of "such things" when she researched conditions in the mills of Lowell for her novel *The Fruit of the Tree*.

13. Eady's position in the village is another expression of the novel's trenchant irony. The grocer's son intent on courting Mattie at the church dance in Chapter I has grown prosperous in the twenty-four years after the crash. The narrator identifies Eady in the prologue as "the rich Irish grocer" (67).

14. The narrator attributes to Mattie's eyes "the bright witch-like stare" which can result from spinal injuries (73). Elizabeth Ammons draws on this association in her reading of *Ethan Frome* as a fairy tale. In *Edith Wharton's Argument with America*, Ammons argues that Mattie begins the novel as a fairy tale princess and ends as a witch who "becomes Zeena's double rather than Ethan's complement" (67). Ammons treats this transformation of Mattie into Zeena as essential to Wharton's criticism of modern American society: "Stated simply, Zeena Frome is the witch that conservative New England will make of unskilled young Mattie; and Wharton's inverted fairy tale about the multiplication of witches in Ethan's life, a story appropriately told by a young man whose job it is to build the future, finally serves as a lesson in sociology. Witches do exist, Wharton's tale says, and the culture creates them" (77).

CHAPTER 5.   NARRATIVE ART

1. Wharton concentrates closely on *Ethan Frome*'s narrative structure in her 1922 introduction, prepared for the publication of the Modern Student's Library Edition of the novel. Her additional commentaries on the novel's art include the essay "The Writing of *Ethan Frome*" (*The Colophon: The Book Collectors' Quarterly*, September 1932) and her autobiography, *A Backward Glance*.

2. Joseph X. Brennan argues that the two characters' responsiveness to nature determines the novel's dominant patterns of imagery, as well as this central division between nature and convention: "It accounts, first of all, for the chief pattern of

contrast which runs throughout this story, that between indoors and outdoors, between the house as symbolic stronghold of moral convention and conformity, and the open countryside as symbolic of natural freedom and passional abandon. And it accounts also for the elaborate system of metaphorical characterization developed in direct relationship to this basic symbolic pattern" (350).

3. This important reference to seeds and fertility is anticipated in Chapter VIII. When Ethan returns from his evening chores following Zeena's discovery of the broken pickle dish, he finds a note written on a page from a seed catalogue: "The kitchen was empty when he came back to it, but his tobacco-pouch and pipe had been laid on the table, and under them was a scrap of paper torn from the back of a seedsman's catalogue, on which three words were written: 'Don't trouble, Ethan'" (129).

4. Kenneth Bernard comments on the suggestiveness of Mattie's name, calling this character the novel's "supreme light image" (180). R. W. B. Lewis also comments on Wharton's choice of this name, hearing in "Mattie Silver" an echo of "Morton Fullerton." In his biography, Lewis points to the ways in which the relationship between Ethan and Mattie "contains memories" of Wharton's affair with Fullerton (310).

CHAPTER 6.   RECEPTION

1. In his biography, Lewis quotes the response of Wharton's long suffering publisher to this claim of inaccurate sales figures. "'Nothing,' Scribner replied patiently, 'is more difficult to meet than the statement of an author's friends who report that a book is selling tremendously or cannot be had at the best bookstores. Retail clerks are very apt to say whatever they think a customer wishes to hear'" (311). Wharton was not mollified.

2. In his 1947 memoir *Portrait of Edith Wharton*, Percy Lubbock supplies another, lighter response to the novel which captures James's play of wit: "I remember one day at Qu'acre, when Howard Sturgis, turning the pages of her latest story (it was *Ethan Frome*), read out a passing remark of the fictitious narrator's—'I had been sent by my employers'; and how Henry caught at the words, with his great round stare of drollery and malice at the suggested image—of Edith sent, and sent by employers!—what a power of invention it implied in her to think of that!" (66–67).

3. Wharton had wearied of this charge long before *Ethan Frome* was published. In a 1904 letter to William Crary Brownell, she complains about reviews for her short story collection *The Descent of Man* which relegate her to the status of James's pupil. "I have never before been discouraged by criticism, because when the critics have found fault with me I have usually abounded in their sense, & seen, as I thought, a way of doing better the next time; but the continued cry that I am an echo of Mr. James (whose books of the last ten years I can't read, much as I delight in the man), & the assumption that the people I write about are not 'real' because they are not navies & char-women, makes me feel rather hopeless. I write about what I see, what I happen to be nearest to, which is surely better than doing cowboys de chic" (*Letters* 91).

4. Sergeant closes her review by assuring her fictional companion that the stories of Jewett ("Queen's Twin," "Dunnet Shepherdess") will "still be full of living

human poetry and truth and the salt-sweet scent of high coast pastures"
when Wharton's novel is "rotting in his grave" (22). In her work *The Critical
Reception of Edith Wharton*, Helen Killoran argues that Sergeant's unflattering
comparison of *Ethan Frome* to the fiction of the local colorists Jewett and Freeman
prompted Wharton's dismissal in her autobiography of writers who saw modern New
England through "rose coloured spectacles" (51). See Chapter 3 for a discussion of
Wharton and local color realism.

5. Most of these early studies make similar reference to Wharton's standing. For
Grant C. Knight, Wharton is "the foremost living American writer of fiction" (338).
For William Lyon Phelps, she is "by common consent" the leading American woman
writer (293).

6. E. L. Miller's 1931 essay "College Entrance Requirements in English: A
Committee Report" includes *Ethan Frome* among the novels assigned at the
twelfth-grade level in American high schools (723).

7. Ransom pays special attention to Wharton's preface to the 1922 edition,
particularly her confession of the difficulty which she faced as she attempted to
mediate between a sophisticated observer and a simple subject. Wharton describes
the problem—and its resolution—in the following manner: "The real merit of my
construction seems to me to lie in a minor detail. I had to find means to bring my
tragedy, in a way at once natural and picture-making, to the knowledge of its
narrator.... Each of my chroniclers contributes to the narrative *just as much as he
or she is capable of* understanding of what, to them, is a complicated and mysterious
case; and only the narrator of the tale has scope enough to see it all, to resolve it back
into simplicity, and to put it in its rightful place among his larger categories" (Lauer
and Wolff xii–xiii).

8. Wharton's biographers Lewis, Wolff and Benstock all testify to her unstinting
generosity. Benstock notes that by the 1930s Wharton was supporting more than two
dozen dependents, "a group that included family members, aged friends, current and
former staff members, war and tuberculosis victims" (438).

9. Between 1980 and 2000, a total of eleven Wharton stories and novels were
adapted for film. For discussion of the adaptation of *Ethan Frome*, see "Edith
Wharton on Film and Television: A History and Filmography" by Scott Marshall
(*Edith Wharton Review* 13) or "Wharton and the Age of Film" by Linda
Costanzo Cahir (*A Historical Guide to Edith Wharton*).

CHAPTER 7. BIBLIOGRAPHIC ESSAY

1. Wharton was consistent in her attempts to focus attention on other novels she
had written. Her godson William Royall Tyler recalls, "She was always impatient
about *Ethan Frome*. She wished that people wouldn't always talk to her about it.
She didn't think of *Ethan Frome* as being her highest achievement or anything like
it" (qtd. in Singley 125).

2. In her 1993 guide to the novel, *Ethan Frome: A Nightmare of Need*, Marlene
Springer points out that the two features which have sparked the most interest since
the novel's publication are its setting and its form (15).

3. Complaints about these errors persist in *Ethan Frome* scholarship. Leach
notes that Ethan would not have begun his day by shaving in the early morning

cold (96); Hamblen points out that the Congregationalists of the 1870s and 1880s would never sponsor the dance which Mattie attends (240). J. D. Thomas' 1953 essay "Marginalia on *Ethan Frome*" catalogues a number of missteps as it develops its argument that Wharton relies on a male narrator who is not credible. Thomas cites confusion over the lumber (alternately "logs" and "tree trunks" in the text) which Ethan brings from his sawmill to Andrew Hale (406), for example, as well as the improbability of the moon rising and setting at roughly the same time two nights in a row (407).

4. Wolff's biography of Wharton also pays generous attention to the details of the French exercise available at the Beinecke Library at Yale. See pp. 157–59 for Wolff's comparison of the "Black Book *Ethan*" and the later novel.

5. I am indebted to my colleague Brian Barbour for his insights into this influential essay.

6. The *Letters of Edith Wharton*, edited by R. W. B. Lewis and Nancy Lewis, is another valuable resource for *Frome* scholars. This collection includes a generous number of letters from the period in which Wharton was writing the novel.

7. In her work *The Critical Reception of Edith Wharton*, Helen Killoran comments on this trend in Wharton criticism: "Since the late seventies critical output on *Ethan Frome* has decreased to an average of about one article per year possibly because, except for feminist theories, *Ethan Frome* fails to respond to many of the currently prevailing critical approaches" (58).

8. A 1979 essay devoted to *Ethan Frome* preceded this highly regarded study of Wharton. See Ammons' paper "Edith Wharton's *Ethan Frome* and the Question of Meaning" in *Studies in American Fiction*.

9. Although this view of the novel is usually attributed to Wolff, it was articulated much earlier than her 1977 biography of Wharton. John Crowe Ransom raises the question in his 1936 essay "Characters and Character," contending that the narrator could not have garnered the story which he tells from conversations with villagers (273). Joseph X. Brennan's 1961 essay "*Ethan Frome*: Structure and Metaphor" treats the visiting engineer's "vision" as "an overt fiction within a fiction" (348). R. B. Hovey's "*Ethan Frome*: A Controversy about Modernizing It" notes Wolff's oversight of Brennan (5).

10. An excellent earlier bibliography is *Edith Wharton and Kate Chopin: A Reference Guide* (1976), compiled by Marlene Springer. Alfred Bendixen's subsequent essays in the *Edith Wharton Newsletter* and the *Edith Wharton Review* are valuable, as is Clare Colquitt's paper "Contradictory Possibilities: Wharton Scholarship 1992–1994" (1995). See also Colquitt's "Bibliographical Essay: Visions and Revisions of Wharton" in Singley's *Historical Guide to Edith Wharton* (2003).

WORKS CITED

Ames, Van Meter. *Aesthetics of the Novel*. New York: Gordian Press, 1966.

Ammons, Elizabeth. *Edith Wharton's Argument with America*. Athens: University of Georgia Press, 1980.

———. "Edith Wharton's *Ethan Frome* and the Question of Meaning." *Studies in American Fiction* 7 (1979): 127–40.

Arnold, Matthew. "Dover Beach." *Victorian Prose and Poetry*. Ed. Lionel Trilling and Harold Bloom. New York: Oxford University Press, 1973.

Baker, Carlos. "Delineation of Life and Character." *Literary History of the United States*. 4th ed. Ed. Robert E. Spiller et al. New York: Macmillan Publishing, 1974. 843–61.

Beach, Joseph Warren. *The Twentieth Century Novel: Studies in Technique*. New York: Appleton-Century-Crofts, 1932.

Bell, Millicent. "Edith Wharton in France." *Wretched Exotic: Essays on Edith Wharton in Europe*. Ed. Katherine Joslin and Alan Price. New York: Peter Lang, 1993. 61–73.

Bendixen, Alfred, ed. "A Guide to Wharton Criticism, 1974–1983." *Edith Wharton Newsletter* 2.2 (1985): 1–8.

———. "Recent Wharton Studies: A Bibliographic Essay." *Edith Wharton Newsletter* 3.2 (1986): 5, 8–9.

———. "The World of Wharton Criticism: A Bibliographic Essay." *Edith Wharton Review* 7.1 (1990): 18–21.

Benstock, Shari. *No Gifts from Chance: A Biography of Edith Wharton*. Austin: University of Texas, 1994.

Bernard, Kenneth. "Imagery and Symbolism in *Ethan Frome*." *College English* 23.3 (1961): 178–84.

Bewley, Marius. "Mrs. Wharton's Mask." *The New York Review of Books* (September 24, 1964): 7–9.

Bjorkman, Edwin. *Voices of To-Morrow: Critical Studies of the New Spirit in Literature*. 1913. Westport, CT: Greenwood Press, 1970.

Blackall, Jean Frantz. "Edith Wharton's Art of Ellipses." *The Journal of Narrative Technique* 17 (1987): 145–59.

———. "The Sledding Accident in *Ethan Frome*." *Studies in Short Fiction* 21.2 (1984): 145–46.

Blankenship, Russell. *American Literature as an Expression of the National Mind*. New York: Holt, Rinehart and Winston, 1931.

Bloom, Harold. "Introduction." *American Naturalism*. Ed. Harold Bloom. Philadelphia: Chelsea House, 2004. 1–19.

Boas, Ralph Philip, and Katherine Burton. *Social Backgrounds of American Literature*. Boston: Little, Brown, and Company, 1933.

Boynton, Percy H. "American Authors of Today v. Edith Wharton." *The English Journal* 12.1 (1932): 24–32.

Brennan, Joseph X. "*Ethan Frome*: Structure and Metaphor." *Modern Fiction Studies* 3 (1961): 347–54.

Brooks, Van Wyck. *New England: Indian Summer 1865–1915*. New York: E. P. Dutton & Company, 1940.

Brown, E. K. "Edith Wharton." *The Art of the Novel: From 1700 to the Present Time*. By Pelham Edgar. New York: Russell & Russell, 1965.

Browning, Robert. *The Ring and the Book*. Ed. Richard D. Altick. London: Penguin Books, 1971.

Bruce, Charles. "Circularity: Theme and Structure in *Ethan Frome*." *Studies and Critiques* 1 (1966): 78–81.

Cahir, Linda Costanzo. "Wharton and the Age of Film." *A Historical Guide to Edith Wharton*. Historical Guides to American Authors. Ed. Carol J. Singley. Oxford: Oxford University Press, 2003. 211–28.

Campbell, Donna M. *Resisting Regionalism: Gender and Naturalism in American Fiction, 1885–1915*. Athens: Ohio University Press, 1997.

Cashman, Sean Dennis. *America in the Gilded Age: From the Death of Lincoln to the Rise of Theodore Roosevelt*. New York: New York University Press, 1984.

Cather, Willa. "Preface." *The Best Stories of Sarah Orne Jewett*. Ed. Willa Cather. Gloucester, MA: Peter Smith, 1959.

Colquitt, Clare. "A Bibliographical Essay: Visions and Revisions of Wharton." *A Historical Guide to Edith Wharton*. Historical Guides to American Authors. Ed. Carol J. Singley. Oxford: Oxford University Press, 2003. 249–80.

———. "Contradictory Possibilities: Wharton Scholarship 1992–1994: A Bibliographical Essay." *Edith Wharton Review* 12.2 (1995): 37–44.

Crane, Stephen. "To Hamlin Garland." March 1893. Eds. R. W. Stallman and Lillian Gilkes. New York: New York University Press, 1960. 14.

Davis, Owen, and Donald Davis. *Ethan Frome: A Dramatization of Edith Wharton's Novel*. New York: Charles Scribner's Sons, 1936.

DeVoto, Bernard. "Introduction." *Ethan Frome*. By Edith Wharton. New York: Charles Scribner's Sons, 1938. v–xviii.

DiNunzio, Mario. "Introduction." *Theodore Roosevelt: An American Mind: Selections from His Writings.* Ed. Mario R. DiNunzio. New York: St. Martin's, 1994. 1–21.

Donovan, Josephine. *After the Fall: The Demeter-Persephone Myth in Wharton, Cather, and Glasgow.* University Park: Pennsylvania State University Press, 1989.

Dreiser, Theodore. *Novels.* New York: Library of America, 1987.

Dwight, Eleanor. *Edith Wharton: An Extraordinary Life.* New York: Harry N. Abrams, 1994.

Eggenschwiler, David. "The Ordered Disorder of *Ethan Frome*." *Studies in the Novel* 9 (1977): 237–46.

"Ethan Frome." Rev. of *Ethan Frome* by Owen Davis and Donald Davis. *The Nation* 142 (February 5, 1936): 167–68.

"Fatal Coasting Accident." *Berkshire Evening Eagle.* March 12, 1904. From *Ethan Frome.* Norton Critical Edition. Ed. Kristin O. Lauer and Cynthia Griffin Wolff. New York: W. W. Norton & Company, 1995. 86–90.

"Feminine Literature." Rev. of *Ethan Frome* by Edith Wharton. *Independent* 71 (November 30, 1911): 1204.

Freeman, Mary E. Wilkins. *A New England Nun and Other Stories.* Ed. Sandra A. Zangarell. New York: Penguin Books, 2000.

Fryer, Judith. *Felicitous Space: The Imaginative Structures of Edith Wharton and Willa Cather.* Chapel Hill: University of North Carolina Press, 1986.

Fussell, Paul. *The Great War and Modern Memory.* New York: Oxford University Press, 1975.

Garland, Hamlin. *Crumbling Idols: Twelve Essays on Art Dealing Chiefly With Literature Painting and the Drama.* Ed. Jane Johnson. Cambridge, MA: Belknap Press of Harvard University Press, 1960.

Gilbert, Sandra M., and Susan Gubar. *No Man's Land: The Place of the Woman Writer in the Twentieth Century.* Vol. 1: *The War of the Words.* New Haven: Yale University Press, 1988.

Gimbel, Wendy. *Edith Wharton: Orphancy and Survival.* Landmark Dissertations in Women's Studies Series. New York: Praeger, 1984.

Goldman, Eric F. *Rendezvous with Destiny.* New York: Alfred A. Knopf, 1970.

Hamblen, Abigail Ann. "Edith Wharton in New England." *The New England Quarterly* 38.2 (1965): 239–44.

Hawthorne, Nathaniel. *Novels.* New York: Library of America, 1983.

——. *Tales and Sketches.* New York: Library of America, 1982.

Hays, Peter L. "First and Last in *Ethan Frome*." *NMAL: Notes on Modern American Literature* 1 (1977): Item #15.

Hobsbawm, Eric. *The Age of Empire: 1875–1914.* New York: Pantheon, 1987.

——. *The Age of Extremes: A History of the World, 1914–1991.* New York: Vintage, 1994.

Hofstadter, Richard. *Social Darwinism in American Thought.* Rev. ed. New York: George Braziller, 1955.

——. *The Age of Reform: From Bryan to F. D. R.* New York: Alfred A. Knopf, 1955.

Hovey, R. B. "*Ethan Frome*: A Controversy about Modernizing It." *American Literary Realism* 19.1 (1986): 4–20.

Howells, William Dean. *Criticism and Fiction and Other Essays*. Ed. Clara Marburg Kirk and Rudolf Kirk. New York: New York University Press, 1959.

——. *The Rise of Silas Lapham*. New York: New American Library, 1963.

James, Henry. "To Edith Wharton." October 25, 1911. *Henry James and Edith Wharton Letters: 1900–1915*. Ed. Lyall H. Powers. New York: Charles Scribner's Sons, 1990.

——. "To Howard Sturgis." October 17, 1904. *Henry James Letters*. Ed. Leon Edel. Vol. 4. Cambridge, MA: Belknap Press of Harvard University Press, 1984. 325–26.

——. *The Letters of Henry James*. 1920. Ed. Percy Lubbock. Vol. 2. New York: Octagon, 1970. 34–35, 123–25.

Jewett, Sarah Orne. *Novels and Stories*. New York: Library of America, 1994.

Kaplan, Fred. *Henry James: The Imagination of Genius: A Biography*. Baltimore: Johns Hopkins University Press, 1992.

Kazin, Alfred. *On Native Grounds: A Study of American Prose Literature from 1890 to the Present*. 1942. Garden City, NY: Doubleday Anchor, 1956.

Keegan, John. *The First World War*. New York: Vintage, 1998.

Kennedy, David M. *Freedom from Fear: The American People in Depression and War, 1929–1945*. New York: Oxford University Press, 1999.

Killoran, Helen. *The Critical Reception of Edith Wharton*. Literary Criticism in Perspective. Rochester, NY: Camden House, 2001.

Knight, Grant C. *The Novel in English*. New York: Richard R. Smith, 1931.

Lauer, Kristin O. and Margaret P. Murray. *Edith Wharton: An Annotated Secondary Bibliography*. New York: Garland Publishing, 1990.

Leach, Nancy R. "New England in the Stories of Edith Wharton." *The New England Quarterly* 30.1 (1957): 90–98.

Leavis, Q. D. *Collected Essays*. Ed. G. Singh. Vol. 2. Cambridge: Cambridge University Press, 1985.

Lehan, Richard. "American Literary Naturalism: The French Connection." *American Naturalism*. Ed. Harold Bloom. Philadelphia: Chelsea House, 2004. 177–201.

Lewis, R. W. B. *Edith Wharton: A Biography*. 1975. New York: Fromm, 1985.

Lovett, Robert Morss. *Edith Wharton*. New York: Robert M. McBride and Company, 1925.

Lubbock, Percy. *Portrait of Edith Wharton*. New York: Appleton-Century-Crofts, 1947.

MacCallan, W. D. "The French Draft of *Ethan Frome*." *Yale University Library Gazette* 27 (1952): 38–47.

Marshall, Scott. "Edith Wharton, Kate Spencer, and Ethan Frome." *Edith Wharton Review* 10.1 (1993): 20–21.

——. "Edith Wharton on Film and Television: A History and Filmography." *Edith Wharton Review* 13.2 (1996): 15–26.

Matthiessen, Francis Otto. *Sarah Orne Jewett*. Gloucester, MA: Peter Smith, 1965.

Miller, E. L. "College Entrance Requirements in English: A Committee Report." *The English Journal* 20.9 (1931): 714–29.

Mitchell, Lee Clark. "Naturalism and the Language of Determinism." *Columbia Literary History of the United States*. Ed. Emory Elliott et al. New York: Columbia University Press, 1988. 525–45.

Murad, Orlene. "Edith Wharton and Ethan Frome." *Modern Language Studies* 13 (1983): 90–103.

Nevius, Blake. *Edith Wharton: A Study of Her Fiction*. Berkeley: University of California Press, 1953.

"New Plays in Manhattan." Rev. of *Ethan Frome* by Owen Davis and Donald Davis. *Time* 27 (February 3, 1936): 25.

Norris, Frank. *The Literary Criticism of Frank Norris*. Ed. Donald Pizer. Austin: University of Texas Press, 1964.

"Owen Davis & Son Help 'Ethan Frome' Tread the Boards." Rev. of *Ethan Frome* by Owen Davis and Donald Davis. *Newsweek* 7 (February 1, 1936): 33.

Parrington, Vernon Louis. *Main Currents in American Thought*. Vol. 3. New York: Harcourt, Brace and Company, 1930.

Pattee, Fred Lewis. *The New American Literature: 1890–1930*. New York: The Century Company, 1930.

Phelps, William Lyon. *The Advance of the English Novel*. New York: Dodd, Mead, and Company, 1916.

Pizer, Donald. *The Theory and Practice of American Literary Naturalism: Selected Essays and Reviews*. Carbondale: Southern Illinois University Press, 1993.

Price, Kenneth M., and Phyllis McBride. "'The Life Apart': Texts and Contexts of Edith Wharton's Love Diary." *American Literature: A Journal of Literary History, Criticism, and Bibliography* 66.4 (1994): 663–88.

Ransom, John Crowe. "Characters and Character: A Note on Fiction." *American Review* 6 (January 1936): 271–88.

"Recent Fiction and the Critics." Rev. of *Ethan Frome* by Edith Wharton. *Current Literature* 52 (January 1912): 112–13.

Reichardt, Mary R. *Mary Wilkins Freeman: A Study of the Short Fiction*. New York: Twayne Publishers, 1997.

Roosevelt, Theodore. "To Edith Newbold Jones Wharton." November 16, 1911. *The Letters of Theodore Roosevelt*. Ed. Elting E. Morison. Vol. 7. Cambridge, MA: Harvard University Press, 1954. 436.

Rose, Alan Henry. "'Such Depths of Sad Initiation': Edith Wharton and New England." *The New England Quarterly* 50.3 (1977): 423–39.

Sergeant, Elizabeth Shepley. "Idealized New England." *New Republic* May 8, 1915: 20–22.

Simpson, Claude M. "Introduction." *The Local Colorists: American Short Stories 1857* Ed. Claude M. Simpson. New York: Harper & Brothers, 1960.

Singley, Carol J. *Edith Wharton: Matters of Mind and Spirit*. Cambridge: Cambridge University Press, 1995.

Smith-Rosenberg, Carroll. *Disorderly Conduct: Visions of Gender in Victorian America*. New York: Alfred A. Knopf, 1985.

Springer, Marlene. *Edith Wharton and Kate Chopin: A Reference Guide*. Boston: G. K. Hall & Company, 1976.

——. *Ethan Frome: A Nightmare of Need*. Twayne's Masterwork Studies. New York: Twayne Publishers, 1993.

Sundquist, Eric J. "Realism and Regionalism." *Columbia Literary History of the United States*. Ed. Emory Elliott et al. New York: Columbia University Press, 1988. 501–24.

Tanner, Tony. *The Reign of Wonder: Naivety and Reality in American Literature.* Cambridge: Cambridge University Press, 1965.

"The Play and Screen." Rev. of *Ethan Frome* by Owen Davis and Donald Davis. *Commonweal* 23 (February 7, 1936): 414.

Thomas, J. D. "Marginalia on *Ethan Frome*." *American Literature* 27 (1953): 405–09.

Tichi, Cecelia. "Emerson, Darwin, and *The Custom of the Country*." *A Historical Guide to Edith Wharton.* Historical Guides to American Authors. Ed. Carol J. Singley. Oxford and New York: Oxford University Press, 2003. 89–114.

Tipple, John. "The Robber Baron in the Gilded Age: Entrepreneur or Iconoclast?" *The Gilded Age: A Reappraisal.* Ed. H. Wayne Morgan. Syracuse: Syracuse University Press, 1963. 14–37.

Trilling, Lionel. "The Morality of Inertia." *A Gathering of Fugitives.* Boston: Beacon Press, 1956. 31–40.

Tuttleton, James W., Kristin O. Lauer, and Margaret P. Murray. *Edith Wharton: The Contemporary Reviews.* New York: Cambridge University Press, 1992.

Van Doren, Carl. *Contemporary American Novelists 1900–1920.* New York: Macmillan, 1922.

Waid, Candace. *Edith Wharton's Letters from the Underworld: Fictions of Women and Writing.* Chapel Hill: University of North Carolina Press, 1991.

Wershoven, Carol. *The Female Intruder in the Novels of Edith Wharton.* Rutherford, NJ: Fairleigh Dickinson University Press, 1982.

Westbrook, Percy. *Acres of Flint: Sarah Orne Jewett and Her Contemporaries.* Rev. ed. Metuchen, NJ: Scarecrow Press, 1981.

Wharton, Edith. *A Backward Glance.* 1933. New York: Charles Scribner's Sons, 1964.

——. "Confessions of a Novelist." *The Atlantic Monthly* 151 (1933): 385–92.

——. *Ethan Frome: A Norton Critical Edition.* Ed. Kristin O. Lauer and Cynthia Griffin Wolff. New York and London: W. W. Norton and Company, 1995.

——. "Foreword." *Ethan Frome: A Dramatization of Edith Wharton's Novel.* By Owen Davis and Donald Davis. New York: Charles Scribner's Sons, 1936. vii–viii.

——. *French Ways and Their Meaning.* New York and London: D. Appleton and Company, 1919.

——. Introduction to the 1922 Edition of *Ethan Frome*. *Ethan Frome.* Norton Critical Edition. Ed. Kristin O. Lauer and Cynthia Griffin Wolff. New York: W. W. Norton & Company, 1995. xi–xiii.

——. "Life and I." *Novellas and Other Writings.* Ed. Cynthia Griffin Wolff. New York: Library of America, 1990.

——. *A Motor-Flight through France.* New York: Charles Scribner's Sons, 1908.

——. *Novellas and Other Writings.* New York: Library of America, 1990.

——. *Novels.* New York: Library of America, 1985.

——. "The Choice." *Century Magazine* 77 (1908): 32–40.

——. *The Letters of Edith Wharton.* Ed. R. W. B. Lewis and Nancy Lewis. New York: Collier-Macmillan, 1988.

White, Barbara A. "Introduction." *Wharton's New England: Seven Stories and Ethan Frome*. Ed. Barbara A. White. Hanover: University of New Hampshire Press, 1995.

Wilson, Edmund. "Justice to Edith Wharton." *The Wound and the Bow: Seven Studies in Literature*. 1941. New York: Farrar, Straus and Giroux, 1978. 159–73.

——. *The Wound and the Bow: Seven Studies in Literature*. 1929. New York: Farrar, Straus and Giroux, 1978.

Wolff, Cynthia Griffin. *A Feast of Words: The Triumph of Edith Wharton*. 1977. Reading, MA: Addison-Wesley, 1995.

Wyatt, Euphemia Van Rensselaer. "The Drama." Rev. of *Ethan Frome* by Owen Davis and Donald Davis. *Catholic World* 142 (March 1936): 723–24.

INDEX

About the Author

SUZANNE J. FOURNIER is Assistant Professor of English at Providence College.